GENERATIONS IN CLAY

GENERATIONS IN CLAY

Pueblo Pottery of the American Southwest

by Alfred E. Dittert, Jr., and Fred Plog

with an Introduction by Patrick T. Houlihan

PUBLISHED BY

Northland Publishing

IN COOPERATION WITH THE
AMERICAN FEDERATION OF ARTS

This book was published in conjunction with the exhibition, *Generations in Clay: Pueblo Pottery of the American Southwest,* which was organized by The American Federation of Arts. The exhibition was made possible by a grant from the National Endowment for the Arts.

COVER: St. Johns Black-on-Red Jar
(courtesy of The Heard Museum)
FRONTISPIECE: Figure 135, Sikyatki Polychrome
BACK COVER: Figure 136, Sikyatki Polychrome

Photo credits:
Al Abrams, p. 58 top
Hillel Burger for the Peabody Museum, Harvard University, Cambridge, Massachusetts, p. 112 top
Edward S. Curtis, p. 31
Bob Hanson for the American Museum of Natural History, New York City, pp. 56 right, 60 top left, 79 bottom, 80 bottom, 83 right, 84 top, 85 right, 91 right, 92 bottom, 99, 112 bottom 118, 126 right
Bob Hanson, New York City, pp. 32, 33 right, 34, 35, 36 top, 37, 38, 39, 40, 41, 44, 45, 46, 47, 48 top left, 49, 50, 51 top, 52, 55, 56 left, 57, 58 bottom, 59, 60 top right and bottom, 61, 62, 63, 64 left, 65, 66, 67, 68, 69, 70 top, 72 left, 81, 84 bottom, 86 bottom, 88, 90 right, 92 top, 94, 96, 110, 111, 113, 114, 115, 116 117, 121, 123, 132 top
The Fred Harvey Fine Arts Collection, The Heard Museum, Phoenix, Arizona, pp. 48 top right, 30, 28, 64 right
The Heard Museum, Phoenix, Arizona, p. 19
Jerry Jacka, Phoenix, Arizona, cover, pp. 33 left, 36 bottom, 48 bottom, 51 bottom, 53, 54, 70 bottom, 71, 72 right, 78, 79 top, 80 top left and right, 82, 83 left, 85 left, 86 top, 87, 89, 90 left, 91 left, 95, 97, 98, 100, 101, 102, 103, 105, 106, 109, 120, 122, 125, 126 left, 127, 128, 129, 130, 131, 132 bottom left and right, 133
Jerry Jacka, Phoenix, Arizona, ©1980, pp. 11, 15, 20, 21, 22, 23, 29, 42, 43

FIRST EDITION
Ninth Printing, 1994
ISBN 0-87358-270-5 softcover
Library of Congress Catalog Card Number 80-81831

Printed in Hong Kong by Sing Cheong

0515/3.5M/6-94

Contents

ACKNOWLEDGMENTS

Within the past few years, a number of major books have been published that survey the American Indian art north of the Rio Grande. These have served to acquaint the general public with an art heritage that has long been too little known except by a few anthropologists, art historians, and private collectors.

Generations in Clay is an attempt to focus attention on a single aspect of native American art — Pueblo pottery of the American Southwest. It is intended to be a comprehensive overview and guide to Pueblo pottery from prehistoric to modern times.

The task of creating *Generations in Clay* has required the support of many individuals and institutions. We are extremely grateful to the following institutions for their generosity in lending to the exhibition that was organized in conjunction with this publication: The American Museum of Natural History, New York; the Arizona State Museum, University of Arizona, Tucson; the Field Museum of Natural History, Chicago; The Heard Museum, Phoenix; the Millicent Rogers Museum, Taos; the Museum of the American Indian, Heye Foundation, New York; the Museum of New Mexico, Santa Fe; the Museum of Northern Arizona, Flagstaff; the Peabody Museum of Archaeology and Ethnology, Harvard University, Cambridge; and the School of American Research, Santa Fe. At each of these institutions, the staffs also contributed generously of their time and expertise in the myriad details associated with this project.

We are also grateful to Mr. and Mrs. Charles Benton of Evanston, Illinois, and Mr. and Mrs. Larry Frank of Arroyo Hondo, New Mexico, who have loaned generously of their collections. As an AFA Trustee, Mr. Benton also played a central role in bringing together The American Federation of Arts with Dr. Patrick T. Houlihan, Guest Curator of the exhibition, and the authors of this book, Dr. Alfred E. Dittert, Jr., Professor, and Dr. Fred Plog, Chairman, Department of Anthropology, Arizona State University, Tempe. In addition, Mr. Benton and the AFA wish to acknowledge the important role of Mr. Bert Van Bork of Evanston, Illinois, in the project's initial conception and early planning.

At The American Federation of Arts, I wish to thank the staff whose dedication and skill made this project a reality, particularly Susanna D'Alton and Jane Tai, who coordinated all aspects of the project, and Konrad G. Kuchel, Jeffery J. Pavelka, Melissa S. Meighan, Carol O'Biso, Merrill Mason, Fran Falkin, and Mary Ann Monet.

We are particularly appreciative of the generous support the exhibition has received from the National Endowment for the Arts.

Finally, I wish to applaud the generations of Pueblo potters who have enriched our lives with their art.

WILDER GREEN, *Director*
The American Federation of Arts

Introduction

"GENERATIONS IN CLAY" refers to nearly two thousand years of pottery-making by Pueblo people in the American Southwest. Here, Pueblo potters, with a background of skills developed over many hundreds of years, have succeeded in producing an enviable record of artistic achievement, one that survives even today as a viable and progressive art form.

Pueblo artists have attained an excellence in form and design comparable to that seen in pottery made throughout the world, even though they work without the aid of such mechanical devices as the potter's wheel or the mold. Economics, trade, the importance of social identity, and pride of heritage have sustained this artistic tradition. Revivals of the art, reinstatements of earlier ceramic styles, and its continuation by younger generations of Puebloans have been encouraged by the imagination and innovation of the potters themselves as well as by the patronage of museums, foundations, and individual collectors in recent years.

Few other classes of objects made by Native Americans have received as much attention as the pottery of Southwestern Indians. Archaeologists who have studied their pottery have divided and labeled it by four descriptive terms that mark chronological units of time: Prehistoric, Protohistoric, Historic, and Modern. These are temporal categories that probably have little meaning to most Puebloans, and yet they have been defined by events that have ultimately altered the course of Pueblo Indian culture, history, and art.

Prehistory is that period of time prior to the arrival of Spanish colonists in 1540. Until then, there was no written record of events in the Southwest. Instead, we are dependent on native oral traditions and on the knowledge gained by the scientific excavations of archaeologists for our understanding of Pueblo culture during this period of time. From scientific research, archaeologists have pieced together the art history of Pueblo pottery, a study heavily concerned with changes in the manufacturing process, with form and design styles, and with the distribution of these traits through time and space. The efforts of such study have resulted in a vast body of literature about Pueblo pottery art.

In recent years, the term "Protohistory" has come into favor among archaeologists working in the Southwest, for it recognizes the inadequacy of time units, such as "Prehistoric" and "Historic," that are defined by the presence or absence of Europeans. Beginning about 1300, the American Southwest saw dramatic changes in its demography. City-states such as those at Chaco Canyon and Mesa Verde were abandoned, and large populations moved to the Rio Grande and other consolidating areas on the Colorado Plateau. These and other changes occurred both before and after the arrival of Spanish colonists from the south in 1540. Hence, the concept of a Protohistoric period from 1300 until 1700 has been increasingly used to refine our understanding of Pueblo history.

By far, some of the most important agents of change during the period of Spanish contact with the Indians of the Southwest were missionaries, government officials, soldiers, and merchant-traders. Pueblo pottery during this Protohistoric period was influenced by the Spanish in both form and design.

The Historic period in Pueblo history encompasses the years from 1700 until 1875. During this time, the era of Spanish rule was succeeded by that of Mexico and finally the United States. In 1890, the railroad penetrated New Mexico, and its impact on Pueblo culture was very significant. For potters, the railroad offered a new tourist market for their wares, and at the same time, it allowed easier access to scholars from other parts of this country and Europe.

The Modern period, since 1875, has seen the transition of pottery-making for native use to pottery-making for sale. Few passages in the ethnographic literature on the subject illustrate this as poignantly as the 1926 statement by Lina, a Zuñi potter and informant to Ruth Bunzel, an anthropologist from Columbia University:

You make many bowls; for the white people you make many bowls. You work a great deal for the white people. Therefore the Zuñi women have something to say about you. So my children said to me. "It's all right for them to talk about you. They have no money. Therefore they talk about you. You don't plant your chile early, therefore they have something to say about you. It's all right. There is still a long time. You will plant it yet." So my husband, my old man, said to me. "It's still far off. The sun is still far off. You will plant your chile yet. Not all the Zuñis have planted yet."[1]

Inherent in an anthropologist's view of art is the assumption that no meaningful appreciation of any society's art is possible without an understanding of the culture in which it is created. This is particularly true for Indian art. For example, color and its meaning in Pueblo art is unique to that culture and cannot be understood by reference to our own culture or to that of other Indian cultures, even those from the Southwest.

For all of the Pueblo Indians, color is the gift of supernatural beings. It has meaning with regard to direction, order of importance, sexual reference, and associations with various animate and inanimate beings as well as sacred deities. Hence, to appreciate the richness of the meaning of color and its use in Pueblo art, one must begin with the culture itself.

The technology of pottery-making is generally passed from older to younger women. For some Pueblo people, notably the northern Tewa, a woman's role is restricted to forming and firing pottery, while men take an active role in painting or otherwise decorating a vessel. Perhaps because it was a woman's art, perhaps because it was an Indian art, or perhaps for other reasons, Pueblo pottery was largely an anonymous art. Except for the last fifty years or so of Pueblo history, we have little or no information regarding the makers of most of the vessels.

With the exception of the information in Bunzel's *The Pueblo Potter,* we know very little about the potter's own view of her art. From Dr. Bunzel's research, we know that what to us is an anonymous art, was to Puebloans very much a known art. Within a given village, everyone knew the other's work — they had to, if only to be able to retrieve their own vessel from a group of food or beverage containers at a communal gathering.

That Pueblo pottery was functional is obvious. Yet we

know from the ethnographic literature that even utility pieces were more than that. Many Pueblo potters anthropomorphize their art: they believe that they do not just manufacture "pots"; they create living things. The Zuñi artist quoted in *The Pueblo Potter* is not painting just the rim or the walls of her vessel; she is embodying a person:

First I paint the stomach and then I paint the lips. I always use different designs on the lips and the stomach. You do not have to use the same number of designs on the lips as you use on the body.[2]

A few years ago I sat in the home of Elizabeth White, a Hopi artist, and while examining one of her highly polished vessels, I rubbed it against my cheek. She saw this and instantly remarked, "Yes, they're my babies!" To Elizabeth White and the many other Pueblo artists like her, their work is an act of creation.

These and other affective dimensions of Pueblo pottery cannot be learned through archaeological excavations. To understand them, one must turn to the written and oral documents of cultures. Yet the archaeologist has recorded most of the tangible record of Pueblo ceramic art.

In this publication, the archaeological record of Pueblo pottery art has been carried forward from prehistoric to modern times, but not in a sequence. It was felt that the newcomer to Indian pottery might best be introduced to the subject through the works of modern Pueblo pottery.

It would be a task of monumental proportions to document by text and illustration every known Pueblo pottery type or the work of every known Pueblo potter. This has not been attempted here. Instead, the authors have sought to outline the history of a Pueblo art form and at the same time to direct the reader's further research and reading. The appendix is an excellent guide to most of the major Pueblo pottery types, with a brief description of design styles not treated in the text or illustrations.

A balance was sought in the selection of pieces for illustration here. The Pueblo pottery types shown are but a part of the story of an evolving artistic tradition. The total archaeological record of Pueblo ceramics will never be complete, for there will always be new discoveries, and it is hoped that there will always be new generations of Pueblo artists at work with clay.

PATRICK T. HOULIHAN

The Southwest
and the Pueblo Area

THE SOUTHWEST as an archaeological and ethnographic entity has been described as the area between Las Vegas, New Mexico, on the east; Las Vegas, Nevada, on the west; Durango, Colorado, on the north; and Durango, Mexico, on the south. Justifications for the western, northern, and eastern margins are not difficult, but the southern boundary of the region poses a problem. Many anthropologists regard the American Southwest as a northern extension of Mesoamerica and argue that any separation of the two is merely a matter of convenience.[3]

Much of the southern part of the Southwest is characterized by the dry conditions of the Sonoran Desert in the west and the Chihuahuan Desert in the east. The two are separated by a narrow strip of mountains and plateaus: the Southern Rockies in the United States and the Sierra Madre Occidental in Mexico. Both deserts have cacti and other plants adapted to dry conditions; high temperatures are common; and eroded block fault mountains are characteristic. In each desert there is a Nile-like river that receives water from precipitation in the higher elevations outside the deserts proper: the Salt–Gila–Lower Colorado River

system in the Sonoran Desert, and the Rio Grande in the Chihuahuan Desert.

North of the deserts a high mountainous belt, called the Mogollon Rim, describes an elongated curve from the southern tip of Nevada southeastward through central Arizona and then joins the Southern Rockies in southwestern New Mexico. The topography of this ribbon-like feature is generally rugged. Elevations in this mountainous belt range from 4,000 to 10,000 feet compared with elevations of 3,500 feet or less in the deserts. Deep canyons and high peaks are common. Pine, fir, and spruce forests predominate, and the run-off from snow melt or precipitation is collected in numerous small streams.

North of this mountainous belt is the Colorado Plateau, an area of relatively flat-lying sedimentary rocks primarily at elevations between 5,000 and 8,000 feet above sea level. Here, variations in topography are due in large part to the action of streams, which form deep canyons that separate the mesas, buttes, and ridge lines. There are districts where volcanic activity has produced high peaks, volcanic necks, and lava or cinder-covered mesas. The San Francisco Peaks

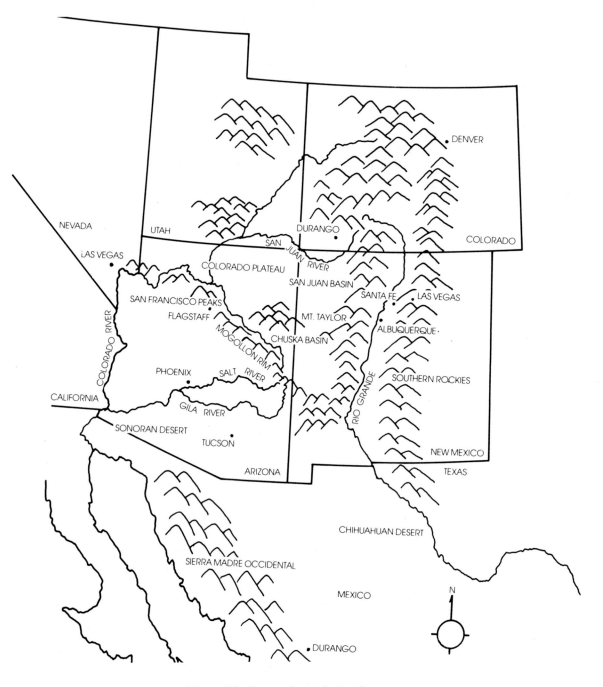

Map 1. The Geography of the Southwest

near Flagstaff, Arizona, and Mt. Taylor in central-western New Mexico are examples. Other mountains were formed where the margins of large basins have been uplifted. The San Juan Basin of northwestern New Mexico and the Chuska Mountains along the Arizona–New Mexico boundary are characteristic of such features.

The vegetation of the Plateau generally occurs in broad bands. Sagebrush plains or grasslands are found on the lower elevations, with pinyon-juniper woodlands at higher elevations and coniferous forests covering the highest lands of the Colorado Plateau. Many of the watercourses in the highest elevations flow for the major part of the year as a result of melt from the winter snows and thunderstorms in the summer. In the pinyon-juniper belt and below, streams are less permanent, except in the northern portion of the Plateau, where the San Juan–Colorado River drainage is the major system.

The Colorado Plateau generally, together with the portion of the mountain belt in the northern half of New Mexico, is the district in which the Pueblo Indians live today and in which their prehistoric ancestors, the Anasazi, once lived. Only the extreme western segment of the Colorado Plateau in northwest Arizona lacked Puebloan groups.

The Southwest is the home of many modern tribal groups other than the Pueblo: the Pima, Papago, and Maricopa of the deserts; the Tarahumara, Apache, and Yavapai of the mountains; and the Navajo, Havasupai, and Utes of the Plateau. Some of these — the Navajo and Apache, for example — are recent arrivals. Others had ancestors who lived in the area. By studying the debris, structures, and artifacts they left, archaeologists have named a variety of prehistoric cultures in the area, such as the Hohokam, Ootam, Hakataya, Sinagua, Mogollon, and Cohonia. The Hohokam of the southern desert and the Mogollon of mountainous central Arizona and New Mexico are especially important to any discussion of the Anasazi, as these groups lived and interacted with the prehistoric Puebloans.

The occupation of the Pueblo area was sporadic in both space and time. Population density varied markedly from place to place and time to time. If the last 2,000 years were collapsed, as in time-lapse photography, a picture of slow but continuous change in population densities would emerge. Before A.D. 1300, there were few areas occupied for more than 100 to 200 years. It was not uncommon, however, for sites to be reoccupied and rebuilt after a period of time when they were uninhabited. Even though there were large centers that grew, prospered for a time, and then declined, the majority of the Pueblo Indians continued to live in small farmsteads with less than ten rooms.

Keeping this enormous spatial and temporal diversity in mind, and noting that developments in the Pueblo area were influenced by peoples and events living elsewhere, one can sketch the broad outlines of human occupation of the area.

Although arguments have been advanced for earlier occupations, the first human activities in the Southwest for which there is adequate evidence began almost 12,000 years ago. At that time, small nomadic bands maintained themselves primarily through a hunting economy. Their remains are best known from "kill sites," where a large mammal such as the mammoth was slain and became a source of food for a short period. Known today as Big Game Hunters, they also ate small game, nuts, berries, and seeds. The most distinctive item of material culture left at "kill sites" is the Clovis point, usually a large lanceolate-shaped projectile point exhibiting fluting on its faces. Scrapers and knives, fleshers, bone tools, and an occasional oval-shaped grinding tool are also found.

CLOVIS POINT

There were few changes in the basic way of life among the Big Game Hunters from the time when Clovis points were made until the end of the tradition in the Southwest some 9,000 years ago. That 5,000-year interval (12,000–7,000

B.C.) was one during which the glaciers were retreating and environments over the Southwest were changing. A succession of large animal forms became extinct, and people came to depend upon different species; the large bison was hunted instead of the mammoth.

FOLSOM POINT

Tools also changed. The Folsom point replaced the Clovis point and was itself superseded by a variety of points classed under the archaeological term, "Plano Tradition." On sites of the Plano period, milling stones, used for grinding vegetable materials, are found. They suggest a greater reliance on plant foods in the later part of this period. Also, many of the herd animals moved eastward into the Great Plains, and peoples who were dependent on them followed. With minor modifications, a Big Game Hunting tradition continued on the Great Plains into historic times.

METATE   MANO

The progressive withdrawal of the Big Game Hunters eastward was accompanied by an expansion of peoples into the Southwest from the Great Basin, from west of the lower Colorado River, and from northwest Mexico. The period has been termed the Archaic, or the period of the Desert Culture. The economy of Desert Culture peoples was based on both hunting and gathering of wild foodstuffs; it was

an economy of total environmental exploitation. The movement of small groups, typically a family of three to eight people, was structured by variation in the availability of resources from season to season. Their travels were scheduled so as to be in a particular district when plant fruiting took place or to take advantage of game animals. Some large sites suggest that congregations of thirty to fifty people lived for periods of up to several weeks where food, fuel, and water were plentiful. This was a time of extended social activities.

Many of the basic economic patterns evident among the Southwestern peoples in recent times have their origin in the Desert Culture. The diverse subsistence pattern, the experimentation with various environmental resources, and, probably, the spread into distinctive regions of the various linguistic families are examples. Maize (corn), first appeared in a primitive form in the Southwest between 4,000 and 5,000 years ago. It had relatively little effect at first except as an addition to the food supply, but ultimately it contributed to the development of large social units. Much like the Apache of the Historic period, Desert Culture peoples probably planted maize in late spring, left it, and then returned in the fall to see if a harvestable crop had grown. After 300 B.C. to A.D. 1, maize became the storable produce that permitted groups to maintain themselves at one place at times when fruiting of wild products was not taking place nearby.

Distinctions in manifestations of the Desert Culture in the Southwest were present from the earliest times. In part, differences were based on the diverse origins of the people. In the western part of the Colorado Plateau, projectile points and other items of material culture had styles that suggest relations to people in the Great Basin. The styles of the "Concho Complex" in eastern Arizona were distinct from these groups and from those living to the south and east. South of the Mogollon Rim, Desert Culture remains have been referred to as Cochise or Southern Picosa Culture, while to the north, the term Oshara or Northern Picosa Culture has been applied. The latter developments were probably most closely related to early period remains along the lower Colorado River. Both the Cochise and Oshara had regional variations that exhibit distinctive changes in material culture through time, especially in the style of chipped stone artifacts. As suggested previously, this distribution may reflect linguistically related peoples.

At least three aspects of the spread of Desert Culture peoples are of major importance to this discussion. First, along the west coast of Mexico there was an alignment of peoples who were related linguistically and connected the Southwest with areas as far south as southern Sinaloa in Mexico. This has been called the Piman Corridor. A number of investigators now believe that the Hohokam of the Sonoran Desert owe their origin to peoples and ideas moving northward along this corridor to southern Arizona between about 300 B.C. and A.D. 300.[4] Among the new cultural traits introduced were cremation of the dead, canal irrigation, villages with large houses, turquoise mosaic jewelry, ground stonework, figurines, and ceramics. The technology of canal irrigation made possible the utilization of areas along the Salt and Gila rivers on a year-round basis. Apparently, there was no conflict with the late Cochise people for resources. For the first several hundred years of their coexistence, there is little evidence of the acceptance of ideas from the Hohokam in surrounding districts, but by A.D. 550, the spread of ideas was apparent. Eventually, Hohokam ceramic designs appeared in modified form on Pueblo pottery.

Second, linguistically related peoples are present today from northern New Mexico southward into Mexico. As early as the Desert Culture and into the early ceramic periods, there were many similarities in sites from the Loma San Gabriel in northern Durango, Mexico, to southern New Mexico. The flow of similar ideas throughout this region was likely, and ceramics are but one of many traits that suggest a unity.

The third aspect of the distribution of Desert Culture populations occurred in the Rio Grande drainage. About 1000 B.C., a variation in the Desert Culture, the Atrisco, is found in the Rio Grande Valley. It has been suggested that the Atrisco is derived from the Cochise, which spread from the south up the Rio Grande and eventually into the Upper San Juan River Basin. This corridor remained intact until at least A.D. 700, and it is along this route that ceramics as well as other traits spread after having been introduced or developed in southwestern New Mexico. For example, brownware pottery appeared in the Upper San Juan River Basin at or shortly after A.D. 1, and brownwares probably preceded the development of grayware in the entire northern part of the Southwest.[5] It is possible that Pueblo pottery has its origin, then, in the early spread of brownware ceramics. And while the forms, paste, and other attributes have changed, the technique of manufacture has remained the same for almost 2,000 years.

Shortly after the time of Christ, the Colorado Plateau was occupied by people known today as the Anasazi. Whether these were new peoples or whether they were the Desert Culture residents of the area beginning to live differently and use different materials, remains a question; probably both occurred. The primary distinction between Desert Culture and early Anasazi populations was the production and use of pottery, but other cultural changes also existed.

At this time, people began to build and live in circular or sub-rectangular "pithouses," the walls of which were the sides of the excavated pit and the roofs of which were made of timbers, branches, and mud. After about A.D. 800, above-ground structures of wood, stone, and adobe were built in bewildering combinations. Although the Anasazi in some districts continued to live in pithouses, the size of the largest Anasazi villages increased from a few dozen rooms to a few hundred and then to over a thousand rooms. These largest sites were exceptional, however; in most times and places, people continued to live in small sites of ten rooms or less. While hunting and gathering remained important and were probably the major source of livelihood for some Anasazi, there were major increases in the use of corn, beans, and squash. The construction of terraces and irrigation ditches to increase yield, and the construction of more sophisticated storage facilities, began at about A.D. 1000–1100.

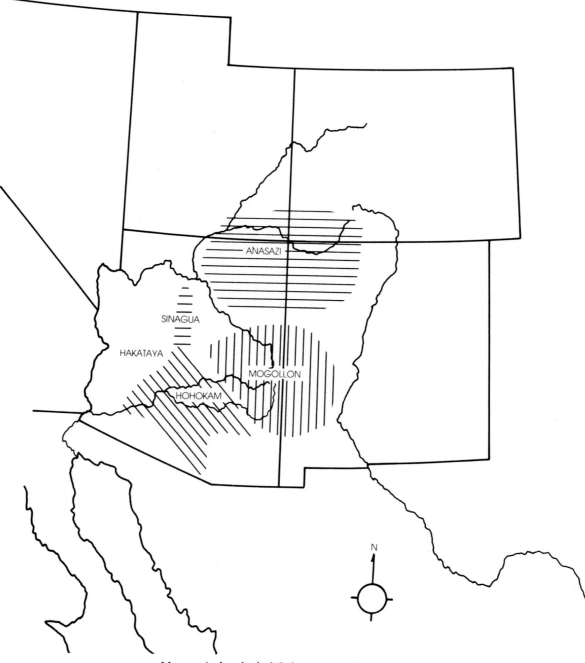

ANASAZI

SINAGUA

HAKATAYA

MOGOLLON

HOHOKAM

N

Map 2. Archaeological Cultures of the Southwest

10

Pueblo Bonito, Chaco Canyon, New Mexico. Prior to A.D. *1000, this was the largest and most impressive Anasazi town.*

At this same time, the cultural diversity of the area increased in two ways. First, the pace of change quickened. Archaeologists working in the area typically define phases or time periods of fifty to two hundred years in length, during which ceramic and architectural styles are relatively similar. This system suddenly proves problematical during this time, however, for too much was happening. Second, small districts with distinctive material styles and developmental histories can be identified. Apparently, highly distinctive local organizations were formed. For these reasons, it is difficult to generalize about the Anasazi of this period.

In contrast to these elements of diversity, there were increasingly strong economic and, perhaps, political ties throughout the area. Evidence of trade is especially impor-

tant. Turquoise, for example, was traded throughout the Anasazi area, and millions of turquoise beads and mosaic blanks were transported to the Aztec and Toltec cities of Mexico.

Evidence of prehistoric political organization is elusive, but there are hints. The large formal towns of Chaco Canyon, for example, contrasted strongly with contemporaneous villages only a few hundred yards away. The apartment complexes of the former were more formal, elaborate, sophisticated, and better constructed. In addition, their inhabitants had far greater quantities of luxury goods. Moreover, satellite villages or "outliers," connected by a system of roads, seem to reflect centralized political control by the inhabitants of the towns. This phenomenon encompassed a large, economically and culturally diverse section of the Colorado Plateau. Such developments did not take place in all districts, nor at the same time.

In the 1200s and 1300s, much of the Anasazi area was "abandoned." Archaeologists still debate the specifics of what happened. While some argue for depopulation, others believe that people simply shifted from a dispersed pattern of settlement to aggregation in far fewer, but much larger, villages and complexes. The reasons for this change are equally controversial. Drought, erosion, disease, warfare, and energy shortages have all been explored. It seems most likely, however, that the abandonment reflected the increasing inability of large, socially complex centers to solve the problems of resource shortages, environmental change, and, perhaps, internal and external social conflict.

The precise boundary between prehistory and history is subject to endless and sterile academic debate. For our purposes, it is sufficient to note that between A.D. 1350 and 1550 the Pueblo were increasingly congregated in large villages and heavily populated districts. In 1539, the first white man, Fray Marcos de Niza, visited the Pueblo. Subsequent *visitas* occurred in 1540 (Coronado), 1581 (Chumascado), and 1582 (Espejo). This last *visita* was the effective beginning of European occupation of the Pueblo world.

Casual and unauthorized colonization of the area began almost immediately, and in 1595, Don Juan de Oñate was given the privilege of leading a colonial effort in the area. A century later, there were no more than three thousand Spanish immigrants to the Pueblo world, but their impact was substantial.

New people bring new diseases, and within two centuries of Spanish arrival, the Pueblo population was reduced by at least two-thirds. Disease was not the only factor; military conflict also contributed. For example, Oñate slaughtered some five hundred inhabitants of Ácoma Pueblo for their refusal to cooperate with colonization. But the Pueblo had their own victories; in 1680 they drove the Spanish from the area. It was not until after repeated efforts in 1688, 1689, 1690, 1692, 1693, and 1694 that the Spanish were able to reassert effective political and religious control over the area.

Ultimately, the Spanish impact was substantial. Economic changes such as herding of cattle and pigs, the care of orchards, and the use of horses and other beasts of burden were introduced to the area. In religion, a blend of Christianity and native Pueblo practices became typical in most communities. Social and political changes remain a subject of controversy among scholars. Some anthropologists and historians argue that the Spanish introduced institutions that centralized political power; others suggest that such institutions had always existed and may have actually been weakened by the Spanish.

Today, the Pueblo Indians live along the drainage of the Rio Grande in the northern half of New Mexico, in western New Mexico, and in northeastern Arizona. In 1970, the Pueblo Indians in New Mexico numbered about 29,336 people; another 6,000 people occupied the Hopi villages in Arizona.

The languages spoken by the Pueblo Indians are diverse and suggest diverse origins for the groups. Keresan is spoken by the pueblos of Ácoma and Laguna in central-western New Mexico; by Zia and Santa Ana pueblos, located along the Rio Jemez, a tributary to the Rio Grande; and by Cochiti, Santo Domingo, and San Felipe pueblos, along the Rio Grande proper. Zuñian, a language closely related to those of some California groups, is spoken at Zuñi, the westernmost pueblo in New Mexico. In northeastern Arizona, the Hopi pueblos, with the exception of Hano, speak dialects grouped under the Uto-Aztecan family tree.

The fourth group is the Tanoan linguistic family, which is composed of the Tiwa, Tewa, and Towa languages. Tiwa is spoken by the pueblos of Taos and Picuris in extreme northern New Mexico and by Sandia and Isleta, which are located near Albuquerque. Tewa is spoken at San Juan, Santa Clara, San Ildefonso, Pojoaque, Nambe, and Tesuque pueblos, which are north of Santa Fe, New Mexico, and by Hano Pueblo in northeastern Arizona. Only one pueblo, Jemez, located along the Rio Jemez upstream from Zia, speaks Towa.

The diversity of social organization among the Pueblo

UTE

UTE

APACHE

NAVAJO

WALAPAI   HAVASUPAI

PUEBLO

MOHAVE   PUEBLO

YAVAPAI   APACHE

YUMA

MARICOPA   APACHE

PIMA

PAPAGO

PAPAGO

TARAHUMARA

N

Map 3. Present-Day Tribal Locations of the Southwest

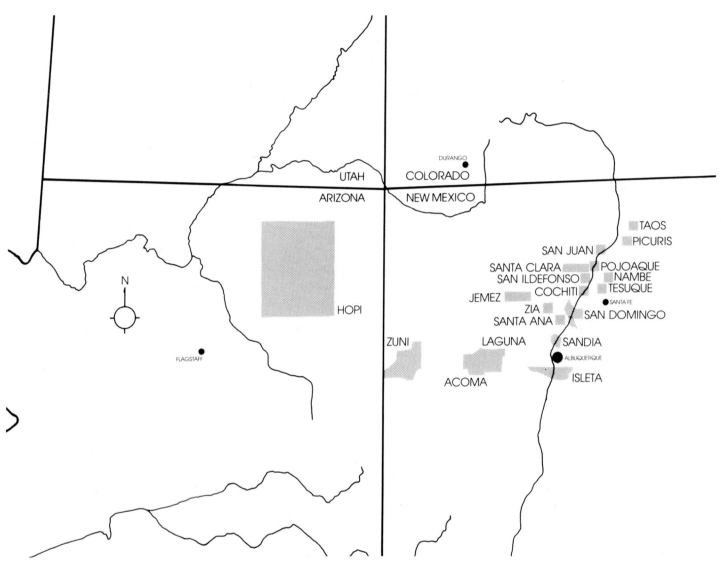

Map 4. Present-Day Pueblos of the Southwest

communities equals the linguistic diversity. Matrilineal clans predominate in the west, while social units called moieties, communities that are divided into two groups on non-kinship criteria, are more common in the east. The kivas, ceremonial structures, are large in number and small in size in the west, while two very large kivas are common in eastern villages. These differences, as well as others, indicate alternative means of decision-making and task organization. The tasks themselves are quite similar: hunting, fishing, gathering, and agriculture were common in all pueblos, as were crafts such as pottery-making and weaving. In contrast with other Southwestern peoples, the Pueblo lived in relatively large apartment or townhouse-like villages.

To understand Pueblo organizational diversity as well as the diversity in ceramics, it is necessary to recall that developments in the Pueblo area did not take place in a vacuum. For many ideas, it is necessary to look to the mountain belt, to the deserts, to the plains east of the Pueblo area, and to the lands of Mesoamerica to the south. The past differences in the availability of raw materials, periods of stress or isolation of peoples, development of complex centers, and large-scale population movements are all factors that have contributed to the differences found today.

Through a philosophy of living in harmony with their universe, the Pueblo and their Anasazi ancestors have successfully survived on the Colorado Plateau for nearly two thousand years. As with any society, however, Pueblo history is one of successes and of failures, of the fragmenting and coming together of particular groups. Certainly, it is a history far more complex than the rough picture that archaeologists are able to sketch using excavated materials. Of those materials, pottery is perhaps the most important. In the succeeding chapters, we will attempt to better understand the Pueblo through a study of this artistic tradition.

Kiva at San Ildefonso, New Mexico. For all of the pueblos, kivas are underground ceremonial chambers that house important religious and social functions.

15

The Study of Pueblo Pottery

STUDENTS OF SOUTHWESTERN INDIAN CULTURES have found a treasure-trove of information, ideas, and conjectures in the study of pottery and potsherds. The technology of pottery — how it was made — and its art style prove to be of equal but sometimes different value. Whatever the interpretive goal of a particular study, the investigator's basic task is sorting sherds and vessels into groups. When those groups are defined according to technological criteria, they are referred to as "wares." The term is flexible, and wares can be separated at different levels. In very simple terms, a distinction between plain and painted wares may suffice. Yet another researcher may separate plainwares into redwares, brownwares, and graywares, while separating painted wares into black-on-white wares, black-on-red wares, and polychromes [many-colored]. Thus, ware names are usually a reference to surface color or a combination of surface and paint colors.

Within the category of wares, "types" are distinguished on the basis of design styles. Because types are defined within wares, sherds and vessels of the same type share a combination of technological and design characteristics.

Type names typically include a place or site name and a brief characterization of the design: Socorro Black-on-white, St. Johns Black-on-red, or Four Mile Polychrome, for example. Both types and wares are defined on the basis of characteristics or attributes of vessels and sherds. Since sherds from even a single pot can and do vary in the attributes used to define types and wares, type definitions necessarily obscure or overlook variation in some attributes.

The transformation of clay into a vessel involves the alteration of materials into a new form. Thus, in the initial instances, production of ceramics was a true invention. Where it occurred, when, under what conditions, and whether or not it happened independently in the New World are questions that will not be considered here. What is important here is the fact that ceramic technology in a variety of forms spread throughout a large portion of the New World.

A sequence of decisions is involved in the selection of raw materials and in pottery production itself. Although many of the alternatives that could have been employed in the Southwest are described here, the reader should not suppose that each potter proceeded independently or individually. If that were the case, recognition of ceramic types, characterization of regional developments, and studies of design style evolution would be impossible. Instead, evidence indicates that the potters acquired a set of ideas about ceramic technology and art from education and experience received as a member of the society in which they lived. Because the training of the potter may have been either very restrictive or may have permitted considerable latitude, there were many differences in ceramic production. Additional variability derived from individuals' perceptions of the "ideal vessel" and their technical skill in executing all aspects of the manufacturing process.

The basic material of a pot is clay, and selecting clay is the initial step in pottery-making. Although clay is a very common material, it is difficult to define precisely because of its varied composition. In a general sense, clay is a fine-grained material composed primarily of crystalline fragments of minerals rich in aluminum and silica. This material becomes plastic when water is added. Clay is found in beds that are formed from the physical and chemical alteration of minerals usually found in igneous rocks such as granite. When the beds are still forming on the parent rock, they are referred to as residual or primary clays. Such deposits are quite different from one another, because of the distinctive chemical components of the parent rock.

When such residual deposits are eroded and the sediments are transported elsewhere (usually by water), they are redeposited in a number of locations such as stream margins, outwash fans, lakes, estuaries, or the ocean depths. Such beds are classed as sedimentary or secondary clays. As movement of the materials takes place, there is a process of sorting and/or mixing with other minerals. Usually, the finer and best sorted clays are those deposited in the ocean at a distance from land. Some of the most extensive clay sources in the Southwest are uplifted beds that were once marine deposits. A major part of the Colorado Plateau is covered by such clay deposits.

More than one kind of clay is available in almost every part of the Southwest, and only experience in the selection of materials yields a desired product. Anna O. Shepard notes that the color of the raw clay itself does not enable the potter to predict that of the fired body. White ceramics, for example, are obtainable from white, neutral gray, or black clays, while buff ceramics can be made from cream, yellow, neutral, gray, black, gray-brown (rare), or brown (rare) clays.[6]

Techniques of firing and the chemical composition are also important to the final color. In spite of the many possible outcomes, sufficient consistency has been developed so that distinctive colors of a vessel can be associated in a general way with the various parts of the Southwest. Buff and brown ceramics tend to be found in the deserts; red-brown and brown colors predominate in the mountains; and gray to white or yellow colors are most common on the Colorado Plateau. The color of the fired vessel is much more varied in the portion of the Pueblo area along the Rio Grande of northern New Mexico, where districts might be characterized by gray, white, buff, yellow, olive, or copper colors.

Pueblo potters today exhibit a variety of standards in the selection of clays. Some individuals continue to work with materials from known beds, using past experience to predict the results. There are records of potters who came to depend upon a certain deposit, and when that deposit was destroyed, gave up pottery-making.[7] Others, using a scientific approach, experiment with clays from widespread sources to determine shrinkage, weight loss, color changes, hardness, and other conditions. This experimental trend appears to have come about partly from exposure by various potters to new and advanced technology in schools. Nevertheless, there remains an emphasis on using raw materials that are characteristic of the native tradition, rather than accepting commercial substitutes.

In the past, most clays were probably obtained near the settlement, but potters sometimes went far afield for special clays. Residents of Ácoma Pueblo describe trips by people from Isleta to mine a hard gray clay, found east of Ácoma. But their activities at such outcrops would be difficult to identify after use ceased for a period of years. Before metal tools were available, if a wooden digging stick was left at the work area, it soon disintegrated, and erosion masked other evidence.

In a few instances, tangible remains existed. Flaked stone picks used to remove clay from seams in the bedrock were discovered during archaeological investigations along the San Juan River, in what is now the reservoir behind the Navajo Dam in northwestern New Mexico. The clay in the seam was black, but fired to a snow-white color similar to that of ceramics recovered from nearby prehistoric sites. Manos and metates, used to grind clay after it was mined, were found near Tonque Pueblo, a late fourteenth- to sixteenth-century ceramic production center in the Galisteo Basin north of Albuquerque, New Mexico. Clay was sometimes obtained by trade, but most makers of ceramics apparently preferred to obtain their own locally. Traditional potters do not mix clays from different sources.

In describing ceramics that were made over many centuries, the question of changes in clay sources becomes central. The length of occupation at most archaeological sites in the Pueblo area appears to have been relatively short. If one assumes that at least part of the ceramics used at a settlement were made there, then the movement of households would mandate that the potter discovered new sources of clay. Records relating to the selection process in a new environment are rare, but an analogy exists in the case of the Navajo, who shifted their area of activity more frequently than did the Pueblo Indians. If clay was gathered from unknown sources, it was moistened and kneaded to test for cohesiveness. Even if this test was satisfactory, the final product may have cracked, but through such experimentation suitable clays were eventually found.[8]

One other factor that may have played a role in decisions about clay was the seasonal movement of peoples between the main pueblo and farming sites. If fields were only a short distance away, the usual clay sources would have been available to the potter, or replacements for broken vessels might have been brought from supplies left at home. But some groups farmed at a considerable distance; Charlie R.

Steen found evidence of temporary Hopi dwellings in Canyon de Chelly, over sixty miles from the Hopi pueblos.[9] Most ceramic manufacture, however, tended to be seasonal and might not have occurred at the farming sites, since tools and other supplies would have been required. Some vessels recovered during investigations near Ácoma suggest that a few temporary replacements were made when the need arose. It is not unlikely that the potters developed familiarity with clays over the area they normally traveled. In southern Arizona, potters among a non-Pueblo group, the Papago, favored one clay but knew how to use raw materials from more than one source. At least twenty deposits of clay in Papagueria are used by modern Papago potters.[10]

Once obtained, clay must be reduced to a state in which it can be moistened throughout. First it is usually ground and sorted to remove foreign materials. Winnowing and regrinding of larger particles assures reduction to a small size. At this point, the clay can be mixed with water, or it may be set aside to dry for future use. The better the water penetrates throughout the particles, the more plastic and workable the material.

A number of potters today who use particularly hard clay from some shale formations soak the tabular pieces in water until a plastic body is created. A curing stage usually follows, in which the clay is kept wet for a period of weeks, or is allowed to dry out and then be ground again at a later date.

Most clays, but not all, require a mixture of non-plastic material, called temper, to reduce shrinkage during the drying and firing processes. Without it, stress develops, because the exterior dries faster than the interior, and cracking can result. Temper may be any substance that does not become plastic when water is added. Vegetable material, sands, crushed rocks, or crushed fragments of pottery are examples of temper used in the Pueblo area; in other parts of the world, crushed coral, crushed shell, bone, and feathers are used. In some instances, vessels used for different purposes at the same site will include different temper. Temper is also a very good indicator of the locality,

Clay in storage at the home of Elizabeth White, Hopi potter

and, in many cases, the time period in which a vessel was made. Sherd temper, for example, could not have been made until there were sherds to grind. Temper, therefore, has become an analytical tool for the study of trade, localized ceramic production centers, and extent of local variation.

The mixture of temper and clay is referred to as paste. After adding temper, the clay must be developed into a given shape. While elsewhere, vessel walls were formed using a paddle and anvil, the Pueblo uniformly shape and thin the walls of a vessel by the coil-and-scrape technique. Although minor variations exist, the technique involves the production of a flat disc of clay, which is then pressed onto a "puki," or support device. This device may be a basket, the bottom of a broken vessel, or an inverted jar from which the bottom had been removed and the interior filled with a mixture of clay and ash, leaving a concave surface for the placement of a clay disc. The wall is then built up by pressing ropes of clay, called fillets, in a coiling manner upon the edge of the disc, and then onto the previous coil. As the wall extends upward, it is thinned by scraping with a shaped potsherd or a piece of gourd, wood, or stone. Today, tin can lids are often used. Expansion or contraction of the

diameter of the body can be controlled by the size of the coil; the diameter of the fillet remains uniform.

Using this construction process, the potter can develop a wide range of forms, beginning with a slightly concave plate, and continuing through shallow bowls, bowls with upright walls, bowls with incurved walls, and jar forms with or without necks. The majority of the shapes produced by Pueblo potters throughout time have been symmetrical, and it has been suggested that the earlier shapes copied basket forms or gourds that people had used before the advent of ceramics. Most of the early asymmetrical shapes found are the result of modeled additions to a basic symmetrical form. Effigy shapes were not found among the Pueblo in a magnitude similar to that of the Hohokam in southern Arizona nor of the Casas Grandes culture in northern Chihuahua, Mexico. Within the Pueblo area, there are only a few shape distinctions with regard to region until the period after A.D. 1300.[11]

As the vessel wall is being finished, a series of decisions are necessary concerning the vessel surface. First, the fillets may be obliterated by scraping, and a few or all may be left to form a decorative band, or a corrugated surface. All of these surface treatments are found on Pueblo vessels.

The surface may be further modified by the addition of a layer of different clay, a slip. The slip may vary in thickness from that of a razor blade to as much as one millimeter. Clay used in the slip is typically higher quality than that from which the vessel wall was formed and may also be different in color. Slipping reaches a height of sophistication just before A.D. 1300. After that date, it was not unusual for potters to apply more than one color of slip to a vessel.

Whether slipped or not, a vessel surface may also be polished. Polishing aligns the clay particles in a single plane, producing a lustrous, mirror-like surface. Among the Pueblo this has generally been done using a small, oval-shaped pebble of a hard, fine-grained stone. Polishing was in use by at least A.D. 700 and is still used today.

After the vessel is finished by some combination of the smoothing-slipping-polishing techniques, the surface is ready to be painted. Black is derived from either mineral

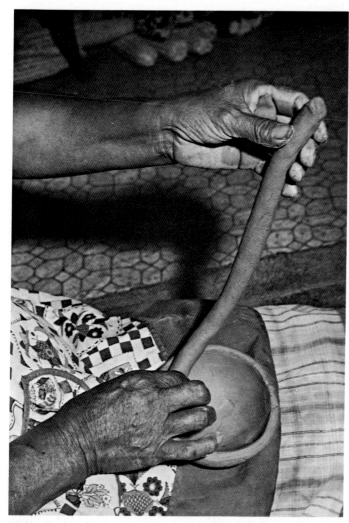

Moist clay is coiled to form the desired shape of the pottery vessel.

The moist coils are "pinched" together to form a rough outline of the piece.

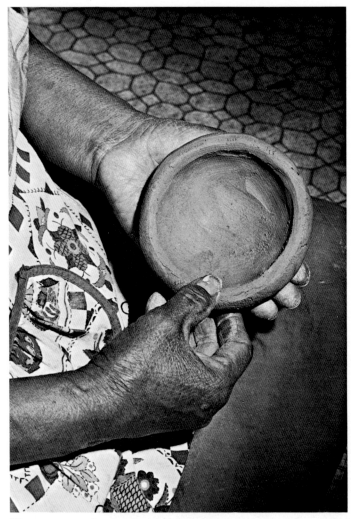

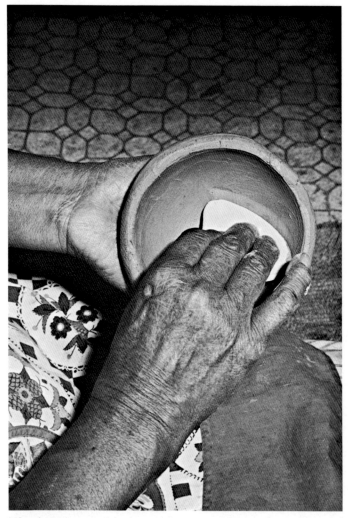

The potter uses her hand and fingers, often dipped in water to aid the process, to further shape the vessel.

The rind of a gourd is then used to scrape the vessel to a finer and more desirable thickness and shape.

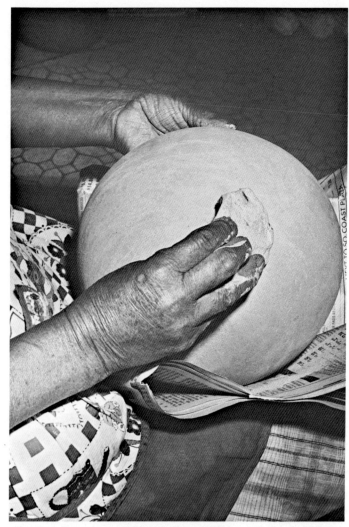

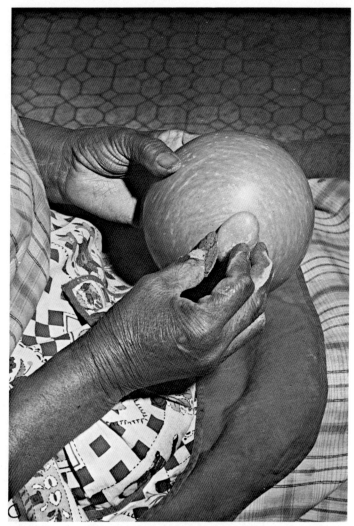

After the pottery is air-dried in the sun or by a stove, the vessel is sanded to a still finer finish with a sandstone, as illustrated here, or with commercial sandpaper.

The pottery is then polished to a fine sheen with a wet polishing stone.

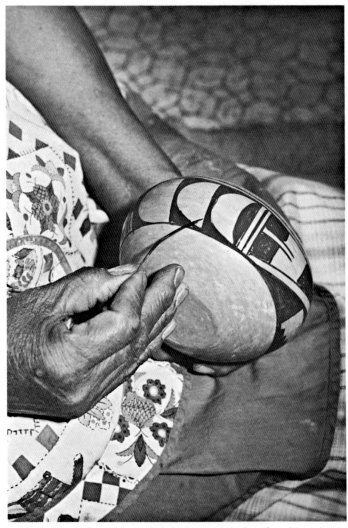

Paint is applied with a strip of yucca leaf that has been drawn through the potter's teeth several times to "work" it to the proper size, shape, and texture. The pottery is now ready for firing.

or vegetable sources. Mineral paints are iron oxides, manganese, or iron-manganese, which, when powdered and mixed with a carrier, produce a pigment that turns black when fired in a reducing atmosphere. Carbon paint is obtained by boiling a plant until it is reduced to a black cake — Rocky Mountain bee plant is the one for which there is most evidence of use. Mixed with water, the pigment will produce a black paint if fired in a reducing atmosphere.

Red colors result from iron oxides that are fired in an oxidizing atmosphere or by the use of iron-rich clays. White can be obtained by painting with kaolin clay. Glazes, used in the Pueblo area after A.D. 1200, are shiny transparent layers covering part or all of the painted surface, and at that time they served purely decorative purposes. They never served as waterproofing, for which they were commonly used in the Old World. Eastern Pueblo glazes have as their base a lead oxide flux with the addition of other minerals that produce different colors; other minerals, especially copper, were more common among Pueblo potters farther west.

Today, paint is applied by the Pueblo Indians to the surface of a vessel using a length of yucca leaf, the end of which has been chewed to loosen the fibers and from which all but enough fibers are removed to form the desired brush width. As in the past, the potter first lays out the design in a drafting technique that outlines the figures. Spaces are then filled in, either with the same pigment or with a different color. Once painted, the vessel is ready to be fired.

Firing consists of heating an excavated basin or kiln in the ground and placing the dried clay vessels on supports such as rocks or potsherds. Large sherds are placed around and over the vessels to protect them from contact with the fuel, which is arranged around them and then ignited. The flow of oxygen is controlled by varying the amount of fuel and the number of protective sherds in the kiln to produce a reducing or an oxidizing atmosphere. An oxidizing atmosphere is one in which oxygen reaches the vessel surface while it is being fired; a reducing atmosphere is one that lacks oxygen.

Most firing temperatures achieved are in the 625°–

950° C. range. Today, fuels often consist of dried dung, but wood is also used and was probably the common fuel of the past. The prehistoric Hopi are known to have used coal.

The last option in the manufacturing process is deciding whether or not a vessel is to be smudged, that is, coated with a dense black layer on one or both surfaces. Interior smudging can be accomplished by removing the vessel from the fire before it has cooled and filling it with organic material such as pine needles. The heat will cause the needles to carbonize and the carbon will be driven into the surface. If the surface had been polished, the result will be an iridescent black finish.

In some pueblos today, the entire vessel or group of vessels is covered with powdered manure at the end of the firing to smudge the complete surface. Painting of the vessel to be smudged will result in differences between the matte black areas that were painted, and the glossy black areas that were polished. Present-day artists also use the process of resist smudging on parts of a vessel, and the part not smudged becomes a field for an engraved design. Smudging was not common in the Pueblo area in earlier periods, but there are examples from the late Protohistoric period of the Upper Rio Grande Valley.

This basic description of ceramic manufacture belies the difficulty actually encountered in studying particular pieces. Temper, for example, can usually be identified only through the use of a hand lens or a microscope; exact temper studies require sawing and grinding a thin section of a sherd, mounting it on a slide, and identifying individual particles by using a polarizing microscope. To investigate firing temperatures and determine the nature of the firing atmosphere, sherds are re-fired in kilns. A variety of physical and chemical techniques, spectroscopes, and nuclear reactors have all been used to identify the sources of clays and tempers. Even using these sophisticated scientific techniques, sherds and vessels can only be classified in groups that are relatively, but not absolutely, similar to one another.

Ceramic design is a more difficult and problematic issue than technology. In part, this difficulty is a reflection of the complexity of decisions that are involved in the creation of a design. A design can involve the manipulation of space on a vessel surface in almost endless variety. Moreover, due to the fundamentally cognitive nature of creativity, design studies remain an area of disagreement among social scientists.

As a result, there are many different perspectives that can and have been taken concerning design. For example, one might take the position that art is "... a type of sensual and symbolic play that is characteristic of adults and in which acts or objects are created and appreciated."[12] This position emphasizes the creative aspect of a design as the potter plays with available symbols to create new ones, or to create original arrangements of old symbols. Were this position true in its most extreme form, there would be little that linked the works of different artists.

Functional interpretations of design have also been made. H. Martin Wobst, for example, has argued that when a large number of people are interacting, a need arises to signal identities, and these signals are carried through material items having stylistic messages.[13] By this view, the design constitutes a regularly structured communication system.[14] As such, style is information and serves to provide identity. Were this view exclusively correct, the artist would be bound by rigid traditions and innovation would be almost impossible.

A third position views art from precisely such a perspective. In his study of Mimbres art, for example, J. J. Brody argues that "... every art object belongs to a tradition; every art tradition is made up of objects in a sequence; the form of each object is predicted by earlier ones in its sequence and predicts the later ones."[15] Mimbres art, he concludes, comes out of a tradition that developed over several hundred years and which borrowed heavily at its beginning from the Hohokam and Mogollon.

A fourth position is reflected in the work of Shepard, who points out that as long as pottery-making was a household craft, its decoration was popular art, representing prevalent standards and average tastes.[16] As such, it was subject to the expressions of the beginner and the inept as well as the skilled person.

Were any of these positions uniquely true, we would learn far less than we do from the study of ceramics. It is from the unique and creative aspects of design that the works of individuals and/or specialists are identified. The use of design to communicate allows us to identify traditions, as well as to identify boundaries between contemporaneous cultures.

Whichever of these points of view motivates a particular piece of research, an attempt is made to group similar designs. Design can be viewed simultaneously at a number of different levels. At the most basic level, designs — especially geometric ones — can be described in terms of the simplest regular parts, which may be termed elements. Kenneth M. Chapman refers to these parts as the basic, irreducible units of design.[17] Examples of elements are a line, a filled triangle, or a hatched band. Only the most simple designs can be separated on the basis of the elements of which they are composed.

In more complex styles, patterning must be identified in typical combinations of elements or their spatial structure, or both. Typical combinations of elements are generally called motifs, although they usually include similar spatial structures or design layouts. Because the layout of a design is critical to the recognition of elements, the term motif will be used here to include both.

A motif is necessarily more varied and distinctive than its elements. In a study at Zuñi, it was found that potters did not think of elements as they are often conceived; rather, motifs were the units with which the potter composes.[18] Shepard points out that it is not always possible to recognize the potter's motif, but she considers it significant when there is repetition of arrangements of elements on the same vessel and the appearance of similar structures among vessels in a group.[19]

A somewhat more formal approach to studying the spatial structure of design uses the concept of symmetry. Designs or motifs on a single vessel may be arranged in respect to one another in a number of quite different ways — as a repeated string, as mirror images, and so on. Symmetry is one quality of design that most readily lends itself to precise definition, since it is based on a mathematically derived spatial arrangement.

The term "style" is used to encompass vessels and sherds that share elements, motifs, and symmetry. Vessels of the same style are similar but rarely identical to one another in any of these areas. Because the same style can be executed on technologically dissimilar vessels, styles can often crosscut wares. On vessels from the Prehistoric period, archaeologists refer to these as "horizon styles," because they were produced during relatively short periods and achieved widespread popularity throughout the Anasazi area.

One fundamental distinction used in analyzing early Anasazi ceramic styles is between "ceramic" and "basketry" styles. Basketry styles in pottery appear to reflect the process of constructing a basket, by beginning the design at the bottom and building up from a circular base. In contrast, ceramic designs begin from the rim down or at least partition the vessel into design fields that are independent of construction or the vessel base. The earliest indigenous styles seem to reflect a basket-derived model rather than the ceramic style already established by the Mogollon. Thus, while basic manufacturing and design skills were certainly learned from the Mogollon, the first locally executed art styles were distinctive. Recalling the earlier discussion of the role of painted symbols in structuring boundaries, the Anasazi seem to say "we are not Mogollon" through their almost certainly explicit selection of a different way of going about the task of design.

This description of decisions that are made in the manufacture of ceramics summarizes a complex technical process and indicates some of the alternatives used in the Pueblo area. Nevertheless, no activity of a group occurs without involving other sociological and ideological considerations and related concepts. These direct all phases of pottery art. They are the conditions under which the craft is learned, the cooperation necessary for accomplishing certain of the goals, and the ritual observances that might accompany the group's activities. Archaeologists are rarely interested in art for art's sake, but study artistic expression to learn about prehistoric societies. Let us briefly consider the diversity and complex interaction of such studies.

Perhaps the basic purpose of examining variation in pottery wares and types is to define cultural boundaries and to date prehistoric events. Subtle changes in art styles through time have given the art historian and the archaeologist keys to chronology, the interaction of the peoples, and the evolution of designs in different regions. A sudden shift in design style and the appearance of distinctive styles or horizon markers are thought to be correlated with changes in social phenomena. When distinctive types are found far from their normal area of production, exchange and trade are indicated.

In addition, there have been attempts to analyze the social and kinship organization of a community by the distribution of certain design elements on ceramics within that settlement.[20] Beyond the community, ceramics have been a means for postulating the form of social interaction of people within a larger district or region.[21] But the interests in a larger territory have been accompanied by the need for a more detailed control of time so that events within the larger area might be equated. One system that has yielded a sensitive order is micro-seriation, in which, for example, change in design is studied in minute detail by measuring the average width of painted lines.[22]

Within an archaeological site, the size and distribution of vessels has been used to estimate the efficiency of food preparation or procurement. The total capacity of vessels found at a site also provides a means of estimating the number of people in a prehistoric household.[23] Similarly, the purpose for which a particular room was used has been postulated on the basis of the presence of particular classes of artifacts.[24]

In this chapter, we have discussed ceramic production as a highly technical body of knowledge and have employed the language and followed the directions of archaeologists and art historians. The sophistication of this approach and the knowledge involved should not prevent our realizing the emotional, even religious base of Pueblo pottery-making.

Traditionally, the Pueblo potter out to gather clay must first ask "Clay Woman" (or "Clay Mother") for permission to take of her being. For example, Zuñi women who gather clay from Corn Mountain believe that "Clay Woman of Corn Mountain gives of her flesh."[25]

When Lucinda of Isleta was learning new styles in pottery from her Laguna neighbor and they went together to get clay and the neighbor taught Lucinda how to ask the Clay Mother for her substance.[26]

In the pages ahead, much of this human dimension is lost to the reader, for it is the dimension of culture that does not remain for hundreds of years in wait for the archaeologists. From the bits and pieces of evidence generated by highly specific studies comes our understanding of the dimensions of Pueblo ceramic art. The personal drama of artistic creation in clay is largely mute, but it had to have once been there. We know this because later generations of Pueblo potters have told us so. We now turn to the pottery of these generations in the Modern period, working backward in time to the pottery of their ancestors.

Pueblo Pottery: The Modern Period

THE LATE 1800s was a period when relatively few Pueblo ceramics were made, and those that were, tended to be inferior to earlier products. This decline of a millennium-old artistic tradition came as a result of a long period of encroachment by non-Indians onto Pueblo lands. Beginning with the Spanish *entrada,* loss of land together with the introduction of new diseases resulted in a significant population decrease among the Pueblos that was not reversed until about 1900. When what is now Arizona and New Mexico became part of the United States, the enacted treaty recognized land grants to Indians previously made under the Mexican government. At first, there was little trespass. But at the end of the Civil War, ex-soldiers began to settle in the West, and some Pueblo lands were lost. Later, in 1887 the Dawes Act and its amendments provided the legal means by which Indian lands could be sold to whites, an opportunity seized upon by the whites to exploit poverty-stricken Pueblos and practiced until 1934.

In addition, there was continued disruption of families and villages because of government-imposed boarding school education. Children were taken away from their homes at the age of six and suddenly thrust into an environment totally different from that of their tribal life. Inherent in these and other such actions were pressures on Puebloans to abandon their customs and adopt the habits of "civilized life." Since then, the various policies have been modified, but the Pueblo people are still faced with the problem of maintaining their heritage while simultaneously adjusting to alien values.

The several revivals of Pueblo ceramic art were a response to the stresses created by the events summarized above. The sale of pottery outside of the pueblos provided a much needed source of income, since most of the utilitarian functions of the craft inside the pueblo had ceased to be important. In only a few years, Pueblo pottery changed from curio sales items to objects of great aesthetic value.

Today, a number of the pueblos have become centers of excellence in the production of ceramics, while others have abandoned the craft or produce very little. Among the western pueblos, outstanding pottery is made on the Hopi reservation, especially on First Mesa at the villages of Hano and Sichomovi. In limited quantity, pottery is also

Indian-land tours, such as this conducted by the Fred Harvey Company, show the change in function of Pueblo pottery from home use to tourist sale.

made at Walpi and Polacca, and an occasional potter can be found in other villages. The pueblo of Zuñi has seen a decline in ceramic production even though a few traditional examples are still being made. There have been short-lived revivals of pottery at Zuñi; for example, modeled owls became popular about 1925. Ácoma, on the other hand, is noted for its technically superior pottery, which is thin-walled, hard, and well-fired. A neighboring pueblo, Laguna, produces pottery similar to that at Ácoma, but the pottery walls tend to be heavier and the vessel forms are less refined.

Of the three pueblos located along the Rio Jemez, Zia is the leader both in quantity and design treatment, even though the vessel walls are heavy. On ceramics that date to about 1800, both Zia and Santa Ana shared similar design styles that have recently diverged. The designs on Zia pottery moved away from the 1800 style, while at Santa Ana the tradition continued, although in a simplified and slightly more massive form. Today, there is very little pottery from Santa Ana. At Jemez Pueblo, there has been little in the way of a unifying theme in ceramics since 1700, the post-Pueblo Rebellion period. The few potters still active there have taken up individual styles that draw upon a number of traditions. Nevertheless, a very recent and exciting ceramic revival has been initiated by Pecos Pueblo descendants who now live at Jemez. The women potters are utilizing raw materials found near Pecos Pueblo and reproducing the old glaze-decorated wares.

Isleta, the southernmost of the Rio Grande Valley pueblos, produces few ceramics beyond a variety of small curio objects. One potter, Stella Teller, does produce exceptional vessels in a Laguna style. Sandia Pueblo, not far to the north, is no longer involved in pottery-making. Similarly, it is believed that San Felipe potters have produced very little since 1700. Santo Domingo and Cochiti pueblos

The Hopi town of Walpi, at dusk. Located on First Mesa, the potters of Walpi have long been influenced by Zuñi and eastern Pueblo pottery.

Hopi Pueblo potter

were once centers for black-on-cream decorated types, and some are still being produced, but the few working potters have become specialized along other lines. At Santo Domingo, pottery-making is oriented toward the curio buyer and is in some cases poorly fired or not fired at all. Cochiti has become famous for the figurines it produces, especially the "Storyteller" forms by Helen Cordero. Tesuque has also departed from the traditional ceramic arts and now produces a garish, hard, and clashing poster-paint decorated pottery that borrows some motifs from older vessels. Nambe Pueblo lost its last potter in the early 1950s and the craft there has not been revived.

San Ildefonso, Santa Clara, and San Juan pueblos may be regarded as the ceramic production centers in the northern Rio Grande Valley. Creativity, excellence of design, and quantity of production have resulted in wide recognition. Less well known, but choice in terms of form and execution, are the plainware ceramics from the northernmost pueblos, Taos and Picuris. These are distinctive because of the golden or copper color of the micaceous paste, which is never slipped.[27] Such vessels are easily recognized by the glittering mica flakes on their surface.

In the Hopi region, many people tend to regard the period from 1650 to 1900 as one characterized by somewhat decadent pottery when the examples of that period are compared with past products. But the "discovery" of the American West by scientists and traders in the 1870s had far-reaching effects. It was during this time that John Wesley Powell visited the Hopi country and collected examples of their ceramics.[28] In 1875, Keams Canyon Trading Post was established just east of First Mesa, and it became the first good market for Hopi pottery. The nearby Hopi village of Polacca was an important source of pottery for the trading post.

One potter at Hano, Nampeyo, responded to the new commercial stimulus and not only produced good pottery but continued to improve it. She and her second husband, Lesou, who was from the pueblo of Walpi, visited nearby ruins, where they collected sherds and copied the designs. Through experimentation, they discovered the clays used for the prehistoric Sikyatki pottery. When J. Walter Fewkes began his work at Sikyatki in 1895, Lesou was one of the workmen he hired. As a result, Lesou and Nampeyo were able to examine over five hundred whole vessels from the excavations, as well as innumerable designs on sherds.

Although copies of the older Sikyatki designs and vessel forms were models for the pottery that Nampeyo produced, her renditions were marked by creative ability and technical mastery. The result was recognition of Nampeyo as an artist who gave to her work a sense of freedom, a flowing quality, by the use of space or open background. Lesou also became adept at painting in the revived Sikyatki style, and after Nampeyo became blind, he continued to decorate the vessels she shaped and polished. Before then, the two had traveled widely, demonstrating the craft.[29] During her life, Nampeyo taught many others to make pottery, but the unique skill she possessed was only rarely surpassed. Today, over twenty-five members of her family make, or have made, ceramics.[30] Many scholars refer to Nampeyo's work and that of her descendants as Hano Polychrome. The use of the village designation, Hano, is important in that it distinguishes these Tewa-descendant potters from other Hopi potters in such communities as Walpi and Polacca.

Nampeyo, a Tewa potter from the village of Hano on First Mesa

31

HANO POLYCHROME. *Ca. 1914. Height 29.3 cm. Diameter 43.2 cm. Marjorie and Charles Benton Collection, Evanston, Ill. This jar, attributed to Nampeyo, shows an influence of designs from earlier ceramics in northeastern Arizona in the bands of negative scrolls.*

FIGURE 15

FIGURE 16

HANO POLYCHROME. *Ca. 1900. Height 20.3 cm. Diameter 30.5 cm. Marjorie and Charles Benton Collection, Evanston, Ill. The arrangement of motifs on this effigy-form borders on the abstract. The absence of a black outline for the large red elements was not common.*

FIGURE 18

FIGURE 17

HANO BLACK-ON-YELLOW. *Ca. 1900. Height 27 cm. Diameter 26.1 cm. Museum of Northern Arizona, Flagstaff. 255/1074. The simple organization of design units on this jar indicates that it was produced during an experimental period when attempts were being made to utilize the Sikyatki style. Red was not used in the decoration of this type. (See appendix, p. 143)*

POLYCHROME JAR, *Dextra Quotskuyva Nampeyo, Hopi Pueblo. Ca. 1975. Height 10.1 cm. Diameter 16.5 cm. Marjorie and Charles Benton Collection, Evanston, Ill. The design on this jar consists of a complex of opposed "bird wing" motifs in which the artist has continued the tradition of elaborate design construction adopted from the earlier Sikyatki Polychrome.*

Following pages:
Fig. 19. POLYCHROME JAR, Fannie Nampeyo, Hopi Pueblo. Ca. 1975. Height 20.3 cm. Diameter 33 cm. Marjorie and Charles Benton Collection, Evanston, Ill. Note the similarity of design on this jar to the one previously illustrated.

Fig. 20. POLACCA POLYCHROME. Ca. 1890. Height 14.5 cm. Diameter 21 cm. The American Museum of Natural History, N.Y. 29.0/259. The decorated surface of this canteen is completely dominated by a kachina representation.

FIGURE 19

34

FIGURE 20

35

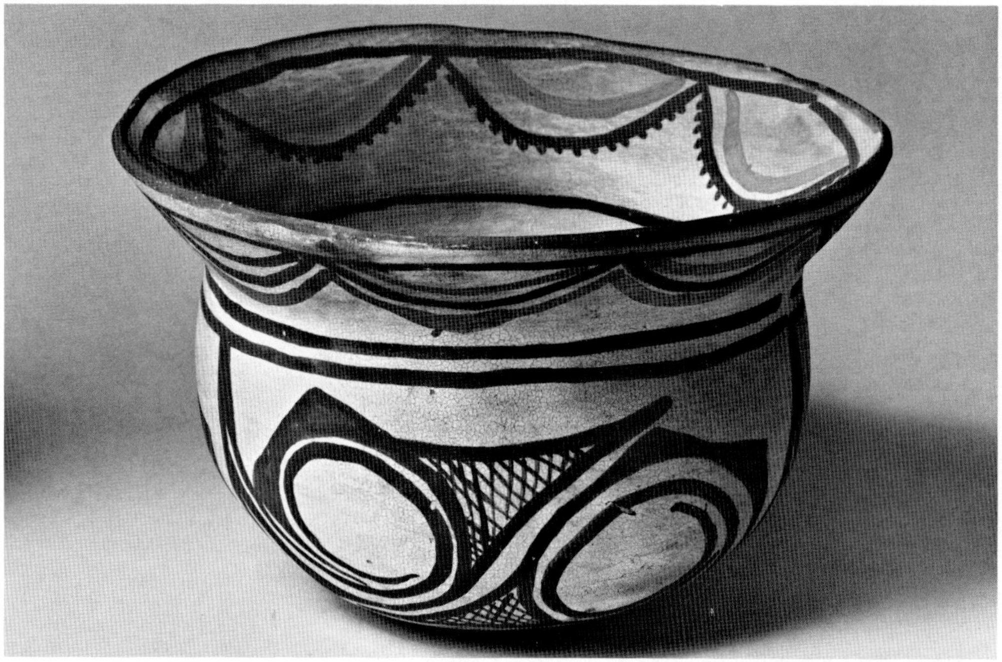

FIGURE 21

Top:
Fig. 21. WALPI POLYCHROME. *Ca. 1880. Height 14 cm. Diameter 21.7 cm. Museum of the American Indian, Heye Foundation. Joel Prescott Heatwole Collection, presented by Mrs. Heatwole. 20/4961. The form of this bowl is deep with a flaring lip. The design motifs appear to be inspired from Zuñi Pueblo.*

Bottom:
Fig. 22. POLACCA POLYCHROME. *Ca. 1800–1850. Height 19.4 cm. Diameter 22.2 cm. Museum of Northern Arizona, Flagstaff. 834/E380. This jar is an early example of the type, as suggested by the use of a band divided into panels. Although heavy, the wing-feather motifs are recognizable, and the depiction of tail feathers is easily seen.*

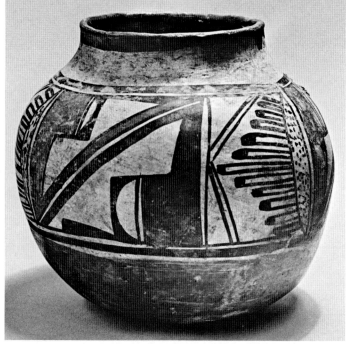

In the Protohistoric and Historic periods there were six large pueblos at Zuñi, which were reduced to only one by the Modern period, although several satellite farming communities were established. As some parts of the older economy gave way to dependence on goods from nearby communities or the government, the vacillations of wider financial conditions began to effect the people. Prices that could be obtained for rare or unusual items tempted some individual potters, and ceremonial vessels or, in some cases, copies eventually began to appear on the market. Vessel shapes as well as surface treatment differed radically from that described elsewhere for Zuñi pottery. Many of these "ceremonial" pieces were covered with a coating of pinyon pitch mixed with fragments of turquoise or turquoise pieces set in a mosaic over the surface. In addition, several vessels had a manufactured hole about three centimeters in diameter near the lower part of the wall, and small holes were drilled near the rim. Fetishes were often laced to the bowl

FIGURE 22

FIGURE 23

Top:

Fig. 23. WALPI POLYCHROME. *Ca. 1930. Height 15.2 cm. Diameter 35.6 cm. Marjorie and Charles Benton Collection, Evanston, Ill. A large kachina mask forms an asymmetrical design on the interior of this bowl, and feather motifs indicate the headdress of the figure.*

Bottom:

Fig. 24. BLACK-ON-CREAM JAR, *Helen Naja (Feather Woman), Hopi Pueblo. Ca. 1975. Height 14 cm. Diameter 20.3 cm. Marjorie and Charles Benton Collection, Evanston, Ill. This jar combines design concepts from earlier black-on-white types in northeastern Arizona.*

FIGURE 24

Following pages:

Fig. 25. POLYCHROME JAR, *Joy Navasie (Frog Woman), Hopi Pueblo. Ca. 1968. Height 24.1 cm. Diameter 25.5 cm. Marjorie and Charles Benton Collection, Evanston, Ill. The decoration on this jar combines concepts derived from Jeddito Stippled and Sikyatki Polychrome.*

Fig. 26. ZUÑI POLYCHROME. *Ca. 1890. Height 35.6 cm. Diameter 30.5 cm. Marjorie and Charles Benton Collection, Evanston, Ill. In this design, arabesque motifs were used to form band divisions and the curved units over the naturalistic deer. The use of a heartline on the deer probably came to the Southwest with the Apache or Navajo.*

37

FIGURE 25

FIGURE 26

39

FIGURE 27

JAR, *Al Colton, Hopi Pueblo. Ca. 1977. Height 14 cm. Diameter 39.4 cm. Marjorie and Charles Benton Collection, Evanston, Ill. This artist is noted for his ceramic creations that combine graceful form and sculptured appliqué — in this case, four modeled corn ears. The influence of his aunt, Elizabeth White, is evident.*

or jar using leather or handspun cotton cordage tied through the holes.

Zuñi Polychrome vessels continued into the 1930s to be modeled after classic pieces last made in the late 1800s. Jar forms differed only in the tendency for the maximum diameter to be relatively higher than the earlier vessels; bowls, however, were made with a flared rim area, which created a new field for design. An arabesque style, executed in a precise manner and highly developed, covered a major part of the vessel surface. Stylized birds characteristic of earlier vessels became lost in the flow of curvilinear elements. Another motif was a naturalistic deer, which was often repeated in a band or framed by an arabesque arc. Frequently, the deer were depicted with a red heart-line, an element that may have been introduced into the Southwest by Athapascan speakers — Navajo and Apache.

A second motif frequently used was a large rosette, which combined some aspects of the arabesque form into a formal pattern. The center usually had a solid dot within a small circle, from which evenly spaced petal-like elements radiated. It is probable that the rosette was adapted from Spanish woodcarvings. In most instances, the heavy rosette was combined with a large but open representation, which H. P. Mera referred to as the "Rain Bird." A balance was achieved that left much of the background undecorated, a characteristic that was in marked contrast to the arabesque style.

Distinctive from the above was a field on which a more complex "Rain Bird" was drawn. In this instance, large stepped areas were hatched, and a solid line wider than the one outlining the "Rain Bird" motif paralleled the perimeter of the figure. Elongated triangles pendant to the framing lines were often filled with red. When red was used in the arabesque design, an entire element or motif was often that color and not outlined; red was more rarely used on vessels with the rosette design. It is not known whether the distinctive styles described represent lines of potters. The uniformity and exclusiveness is suggestive of individualism rather than of developmental process.

Ceramic production at Zuñi decreased dramatically at the turn of the century. Revival efforts produced vessels with applique figures of frogs, dragonflies, butterflies, and

FIGURE 28

ZUÑI POLYCHROME. *Ca. 1890. Height 16.5 cm. Diameter 42 cm. Marjorie and Charles Benton Collection, Evanston, Ill. The flaring rim bowls of this type are similar in shape to Walpi Polychrome. The decoration on the interior of this bowl shows the distinctive arabesque style.*

FIGURE 30

FIGURE 29

ZUÑI POLYCHROME. *Ca. 1885. Height 25.4 cm. Diameter 35.6 cm. Marjorie and Charles Benton Collection, Evanston, Ill. A large rosette, possibly of Spanish origin, dominates the design on this jar, while the small arabesque birds and thin volutes play a minor role.*

ZUÑI POLYCHROME. *Ca. 1890. Height 22.4 cm. Diameter 28 cm. Marjorie and Charles Benton Collection, Evanston, Ill. This jar depicts the "Rain Bird," one of four styles used during this period, when the most sophisticated examples of this type were produced. The hatching on the design motif and the scroll that becomes the bird's head resembles Tularosa Black-on-white.*

Ácoma Pueblo, New Mexico. Called the "Sky City," Ácoma has been continuously occupied since A.D. *1200.*

Street scene at Ácoma Pueblo, New Mexico

Laguna Pueblo. The residents of Laguna Pueblo are closely associated with Ácoma. They speak the same language and over the years have shared much of their ceramic art.

other life forms, but with little in the way of brushwork. A second direction during these revivals utilized elements from older vessels but in a heavy and widely-spaced pattern. Draftsmanship showed a distinct decline.[31]

By the beginning of the Modern period, only two pueblos, Ácoma and Laguna, remained from the many hundreds that once were scattered over the area between Zuñi and the Rio Grande. Even though Ácoma continued as a focal point where people returned for ceremonies and other purposes, it started to lose its role as a primary place of residence as an increasing number of its members began to build their homes along the Rio San Jose, where only seasonally occupied structures once existed. Soon, Indian-White interaction became centered around the settlements of Acomita and McCartys, leaving Ácoma with few permanent residents, unspoiled by many modern innovations.

Laguna Pueblo has had a somewhat different history. Beginning as a seasonal farming site used by Ácoma people, it became the rallying point for many families displaced by the Pueblo Rebellion of 1680 and grew rapidly. Differences of opinions among the diverse factions, however, soon resulted in splinter groups who moved away from the center and established semi-autonomous villages. Although Mesita, New Laguna, Casa Blanca, Seama, and the other settlements remained within the Laguna sphere, they were more independent than the Ácoma satellites. If pottery-making had continued as an important art form there, it might have displayed distinctions among the several villages. Unfortunately, production began to decline shortly after the beginning of the Modern period, and almost no pottery has been made since 1920.

Among Ácoma potters, styles from the Historic period evolved into what has been termed Ácoma Polychrome at a time almost coincident with the beginning of the Modern period. Larry Frank and Francis H. Harlow recognized changes that included modifications in vessel shape, in the paste, and in decorations.[32] Jar forms showed little definition between body sections; the divisions were joined by smooth curves, and the maximum body diameter was slightly higher. The walls became thinner again, and the paste was more likely to be white. Embellishments more often included birds and floral motifs, which were executed

FIGURE 34   FIGURE 35

FIGURE 36

Top left:
Fig. 34. ÁCOMA POLYCHROME. Ca. 1885. Height 29.2 cm. Diameter 30.5 cm. Marjorie and Charles Benton Collection, Evanston, Ill. This jar displays a pattern of design element reversal. Instead of being opposed to the interlocked hatched elements, the solid rectilinear scrolls have been turned outward.

Top right:
Fig. 35. ÁCOMA POLYCHROME. Ca. 1890. Height 30.5 cm. Diameter 36.8 cm. Marjorie and Charles Benton Collection, Evanston, Ill. The entire field of this jar has been partitioned by a grid, and each square includes a similar asymmetrical design. Diagonal bands have been created by reversing the design within adjacent squares.

Bottom:
Fig. 36. ÁCOMA POLYCHROME. Ca. 1880. Height 31.8 cm. Diameter 36.8 cm. Marjorie and Charles Benton Collection, Evanston, Ill. Even in pre-Spanish times, there was a trade route between Ácoma and Zia Pueblo. The extent of contact is often indicated in borrowed ceramic design elements. Here, the curved band of red and orange stripes is a Zia motif incorporated into an Ácoma pattern.

FIGURE 37

FIGURE 38

ÁCOMA POLYCHROME. *Ca. 1890. Height 21.6 cm. Diameter 26.7 cm. Marjorie and Charles Benton Collection, Evanston, Ill. Many Ácoma jars produced for commercial distribution in the late 1800s gave the impression of mechanical repetition of design units, which were derived from a variety of sources. Hopi, Cibola White Ware, and Rio Grande motifs have been assembled in the pattern on this jar.*

ÁCOMA POLYCHROME. *Ca. 1900. Height 28 cm. Diameter 30.5 cm. Marjorie and Charles Benton Collection, Evanston, Ill. These bird forms were found on many Ácoma vessels between 1900 and 1930, but in general, the use of multiple paneled bands repeating naturalistic bird figures was a style infrequently found on this type.*

carefully, but in a free and informal style. Almost all examples retained some elements from the earlier arabesque swirls, and there was frequent repetition of small hatched forms.

The quality and attractiveness of Ácoma pottery made it quickly popular among the growing tourist/collector markets of the early 1900s. Possibly as a result of success with a particular range of designs, little change is evident until the 1930s. During the Great Depression, sales dropped and the craft began to decline. It was at this time that Dr. Kenneth M. Chapman, under the auspices of the Indian Arts Fund, purchased pottery at various pueblos and encouraged the continuation of the art. Experimentation by some Ácoma potters led to a style that emphasized a single

motif, such as a bird or deer on a plain background, or one with very little other painting. Fortunately, the architectural style of the modern American home of that period was marked by austere lines and simplicity of decor. Ácoma potters found a ready market among interior decorators, but this revival was interrupted by World War II.

Among the important post–World War II events that stimulated ceramic production among Ácoma women was the dramatic increase in tourism in the Southwest and the rising value of art objects, hand-crafted items, and antiques. At various Southwestern fairs and markets, prize-winning pottery began to bring higher and higher returns because of quality and the potential for future price increases. Many individuals considered the purchase of high quality crafts and works of art as the best investment that they could make, and today their expectations have been realized. This

FIGURE 39

BLACK-ON-WHITE JAR, *Lucy M. Lewis, Ácoma Pueblo. 1972. Height 26.7 cm. Diameter 24.1 cm. Marjorie and Charles Benton Collection, Evanston, Ill. Lucy Lewis is noted for her great versatility in controlling art styles and for the graceful forms of her vessels. Her talent is demonstrated on this jar, where she has drawn two registers of hatched, non-interlocking zigzag frets.*

popularity also made identity symbols important as potters became known. Earlier pieces might have simply had "Ácoma" painted on the base, but now the signature of the potters as well as distinctive designs produced by particular individuals appeared on vessels. The effect was much the same as a signed oil painting and, in many respects, represented conditions similar to the distinctive style developments of the thirteenth and fourteenth centuries.

The components involved in the emphasis on identity are, in large part, conjectural. At least some reasons

FIGURE 40

BLACK-ON-WHITE JAR, *Marie Z. Chino, Ácoma Pueblo. Ca. 1970. Height 22.9 cm. Diameter 20.3 cm. Marjorie and Charles Benton Collection, Evanston, Ill. This jar has been decorated with an all-over pattern using a maze of interlocking frets.*

involved economics and the borrowing of American symbols, since those with which the Pueblo people were familiar might not have been recognized by non-Pueblo members. The use of symbols that could be interpreted by others may also have been the result of increasing exposure to national and international events and the Indian Land Claim Act. At the time that Ácoma Pueblo was attempting to validate a claim to its earlier lands, Reynold J. Ruppe and Alfred E. Dittert were in the vicinity studying archaeological remains related to Ácoma prehistory. Remembering Chapman's encouragement to maintain the Ácoma style, women potters asked them for designs that the Old

FIGURE 41

POLYCHROME CANTEEN, *Pablita Concho (Feather Woman),* *Ácoma Pueblo. Ca. 1970. Height 15.2 cm. Diameter 15.2 cm. Marjorie and Charles Benton Collection, Evanston, Ill. This canteen has been decorated with an opposed hatched and curvilinear scroll design, which was adapted from that of Tularosa Black-on-white.*

People had used. These were provided, and designs that revived styles from Tularosa Black-on-white and other local prehistoric types soon began to appear. Today, decorative forms from a variety of non-local types are being used, but in a rendition that is distinctly from Ácoma.

Although Ácoma potters did not receive the early acclaim that Nampeyo did, the post–World War II years brought recognition to many excellent artists and craftswomen. Among those who have become known widely are Lucy M. Lewis and her daughters, and Marie Z. Chino and her daughters. Other potters of note include Pablita Concho, Jessie Garcia and her daughters, Juana Leno, and Mary Ann Hampton. While the styles developed through experimentation differ among the households, the distinctive thin wall, white paste, and well-fired characteristics of the Ácoma vessels remain in common. Other motifs that have come into use but are non-Ácoma in their origin include Mimbres figures, a version of the Zuñi deer with a heartline, and an intricate fine-line design resembling the floated twill of a basket.

It is not possible to see general ceramic changes in the Rio Grande region during the Modern period Each of the pueblos had become individualistic; in some the craft declined and disappeared, while in others it became an advanced art. There is a temptation to view the diversification among the pueblos today as an analogous situation to what may have taken place prehistorically when specialized centers were believed to have come into existence. The reasons for variety certainly are different, but parallels exist in the competition for trade, even though the type of market and function of pottery has changed.

The ceramic style brought back from El Paso by Isleta Pueblo people when they returned with the Spanish in 1692, following the Pueblo Rebellion, seems to have been maintained into the 1800s. Unfortunately, little is known about Isleta's pottery production during the Historic period, and some vessels thought to have been made at Isleta might have been products of nearby Spanish-American communities. That some specialized pottery was being produced that may not have reached the market is suggested by the assertion of elder Ácoma people that Isleta people came to the Ácoma region for clay when certain kinds of pottery were desired. The recent Isleta ceramics are limited to curio objects made with a brown to tan local clay. As minimal as is the knowledge about Isleta pottery, even less is known about Sandia Pueblo. Apparently, the craft has been almost nonexistent there since the mid-1700s.

Jemez Pueblo also seemed to have discontinued decorated pottery after 1750. Nevertheless, utility wares were

FIGURE 42

FIGURE 44

Top left:
Fig. 42. BLACK-ON-WHITE JAR, *Sarah Garcia, Ácoma Pueblo. Ca. 1970. Height 22.9 cm. Diameter 24.1 cm. Marjorie and Charles Benton Collection, Evanston, Ill. In the design on this traditional jar form, the artist has sharply contrasted two fields by using an almost negative style in the lower band and a simple, open decoration above.*

Top right:
Isleta Pueblo potter

Bottom:
Fig. 44. LAGUNA POLYCHROME, *Evelyn Cheromiah. Ca. 1977. Height 28.6 cm. Diameter 39.4 cm. The Heard Museum, Phoenix, Ariz. NA-SW-LA-A7-3. This vessel was an award-winner at The Heard Museum Guild's Annual Arts and Crafts Exhibit in 1978. The design incorporates many elements associated with Ácoma Pueblo.*

FIGURE 46

FIGURE 45

ZIA POLYCHROME. *Ca. 1900. Height 21.6 cm. Diameter 30.5 cm. Marjorie and Charles Benton Collection, Ill. The paste of this jar indicates a Zia Pueblo origin, but the shape and design are suggestive of early Ácoma Polychrome.*

ZIA POLYCHROME. *Ca. 1875. Height 45.7 cm. Diameter 53.3 cm. Marjorie and Charles Benton Collection, Evanston, Ill. The use of red as seen in the feathers, terraced figures, and broad curved band on this jar was frequently a major aspect of designs of this type.*

made, and since the early part of the twentieth century, several attempts to revive decorated wares have occurred. One woman, attempting to simulate old glazes, decorated vessels with pinyon pitch after they had been fired. Reheating set the pinyon pitch and produced glossy areas. The type did not become popular, and few pieces survive. Similarly, some ceramics were made using black carbon paint on an unslipped surface. Firing the pottery in a reducing atmosphere resulted in a grayish-brown background, a style that was not attractive to the market. Far more popular as a curio item were the poster-paint decorated vessels still being produced in small quantities. In spite of the seemingly sporadic nature of the tradition, good potters are still present in Jemez, and the craft continues to be taught. The most attractive and artistically excellent products are the

result of a very recent ceramic revival among Jemez potters.

Because of disease and Plains Indian raids, Pecos Pueblo was abandoned in 1838 by its last seventeen survivors, who moved to Jemez to join their relatives. Today, Pecos is a national monument, and a volunteer there, Lois Wittich Giles, began a systematic search for the clays that might have been used by the Pecos women. She also analyzed the glaze paint and devised a formula by which the glaze could be produced. At this point, a potter from Jemez, Evelyn Vigil, was encouraged to work with the materials and continue experimentation with the old Pecos glaze style ceramics. She continued to search for clays and worked with the materials until the proper combinations were obtained. Today, after five years of effort, Evelyn Vigil and Juanita Toledo are producing outstanding pottery.[33]

FIGURE 47

FIGURE 48

Top:
Fig. 47. ZIA POLYCHROME. *Ca. 1915. Height 24.1 cm. Diameter 45.7 cm. Marjorie and Charles Benton Collection, Evanston, Ill. The band on this dough-mixing bowl is almost identical in design to many bowls of this type. The interior has been slipped with red but left undecorated.*

Bottom:
Fig. 48. ZIA POLYCHROME. *Ca. 1920. Height 39.4 cm. Diameter 43.2 cm. Marjorie and Charles Benton Collection, Evanston, Ill. The shape of this jar and the motifs used in its decoration are distinctively of Zia Pueblo origin, but the style is very similar to Santo Domingo Polychrome.*

At the beginning of the Modern period, Zia Polychrome was already being made at Zia. Changes from preceding types were subtle but became more pronounced through time. Jar forms tended to be less spherical and eventually developed a high shoulder, so that there was an increasing change to a straight or even concave lower body wall. A much better polish came into being on the lower wall, and the white slip used in the area of decoration became hard and glossy. The introduction of realistic floral motifs and birds took the place of the earlier bird-like swirls. In some recent pieces, red-slipped bases replace the red band.[34] One outstanding potter making the traditional style is Lucinda Torribio.

A recent innovation by Sofia and Rafael Medina at Zia is the manufacture of large jars using traditional techniques and shapes. After the vessel is fired, it is decorated with acrylic paint. Motifs include small birds with volute tails, stylized floral designs, the Zia sun symbol mask, and similar details from older designs. Nevertheless, these older designs have become subsidiary to extremely elaborate figures of animals, dancers, and other personages from Zia culture, portrayed in vivid colors and minute detail. Usu-

FIGURE 49

FIGURE 50

Top:

Fig. 49. ZIA POLYCHROME, Sophia Medina. Ca. 1965. Height 31.7 cm. Diameter 34.3 cm. Marjorie and Charles Benton Collection, Evanston, Ill. On this jar, the artist has used naturalistic birds in opposed units, framed by the broadline band that is characteristic of Zia styles on one set and by the sun symbol on the other.

Bottom:

Fig. 50. ZIA ACRYLIC, Sophia and Rafael Medina. Ca. 1970. Height 28 cm. Diameter 31.7 cm. The Heard Museum, Phoenix, Ariz. NA-SW-Z1-A12-1. The use of acrylic paint on their vessels is unique to these two artists at Zia Pueblo.

Following pages:

Fig. 51. ZIA POLYCHROME. Ca. 1915. Height 44.4 cm. Diameter 50.8 cm. Marjorie and Charles Benton Collection, Evanston, Ill. Naturalistic deer and bird motifs came into use in the late 1800s, but unlike those found on Zuñi vessels, the heartline in the deer motif was rarely used on Zia pottery.

Fig. 52. SANTA ANA POLYCHROME. Ca. 1870–1890. Height 16 cm. Diameter 17.5 cm. The Millicent Rogers Museum, Taos, N. Mex. PO-109. The realistic antelope figure in a natural setting and the form of a pitcher are both unusual for Santa Ana pottery.

ally the background is white or black and the motifs stand out in sharp contrast.

The Modern period at Santa Ana was much less innovative, since Santa Ana Polychrome differed in few respects from earlier types. Jar bodies were globular but with a pronounced neck. Designs were dominated by large areas of red, not always outlined with black. A type of negative element was created when space was left open within the red area and the slip became the color element. For a time, pottery-making seemed to have almost disappeared, until Dora Montoya began to make pieces that continued the old style.[35] Elements are not as bold but include broad lines, scallops, and heavy curved triangular forms in black or red outlined with a thin black line. The decorated area is less than the background area.[36]

San Felipe Pueblo has been characterized earlier as a pueblo that continued to produce good utility ware but no decorated types after 1700. Claims have been made that

FIGURE 51

52

FIGURE 52

53

FIGURE 53

some pieces obtained at San Felipe were the products of potters there, but characteristics of decoration and physical attributes suggest other sources. Stanley A. Stubbs recorded a few small-scale attempts to revive the craft, none of which proved ultimately successful.

Quite different from the dearth of pottery-making at San Felipe is the recent history of production at Santo Domingo and Cochiti.[37] Although Santo Domingo has been identified as one of the most conservative pueblos, it has a reputation for intensive trading of craft goods. The simultaneous production of pieces that maintain the quality of traditional styles, and of others that are almost purely curio pieces, exemplifies this contrast. Similarly, some styles are distinctive of Santo Domingo, while others are borrowed from other pueblos. At one extreme are local polychromes and at the other are black-on-black pieces inspired by the success of some Tewa pueblos.

Also intriguing is the coexistence of at least two entirely distinct modes of expression in Santo Domingo pottery of the Modern period. One is a continuation of Kiua Polychrome, with formalized banding, usually divided into

Top:

Fig. 53. SANTA ANA POLYCHROME. *Ca. 1820–1880. Height 26.7 cm. Diameter 28 cm. Fred Harvey Collection, The Heard Museum, Phoenix, Ariz. 90-P. The use of broad red elements framed by black lines separates this jar from Zia Polychrome. The design on the far left has been referred to as the "Eiffel Tower" figure.*

Bottom:

Fig. 54. SANTA ANA POLYCHROME. *Ca. 1890. Height 25.4 cm. Diameter 40.6 cm. Fred Harvey Collection, The Heard Museum, Phoenix, Ariz. 102-P. On this bowl, the broad line-work is reminiscent of the "rainbow" design common to Zia Polychrome.*

FIGURE 54

FIGURE 55

panels containing geometrics. The other is the stylistically freer Santo Domingo Polychrome. Jars of the latter type are close to cylindrical, stilted banding breaks down, and motifs include rather heavy birds and floral forms. Red is often included in the motifs, whereas in the past it has been confined to the base of Kiua Polychrome vessels.

Elements from Santo Domingo Polychrome are found most frequently, but not exclusively, on commercial pieces, where they are applied in a rather slipshod method. Most recently, the black, brown, gray, and white colors have been produced by the use of poor-quality oil paint.[38] On the other hand, excellent works have been produced using a negative style where black and/or red are the dominant colors and the cream background shows through as thin lines. The Kiua Polychrome style is also used in black-on-red and black-on-black forms. Among the well-known Santo Domingo Modern period artists are Santana Melcher, Crucita Melcher, Crucita Herrera Coriz, and Lupe Tenoria.

Santo Domingo and Cochiti developed their own distinct versions of Kiua Polychrome by 1880. At that time, paneling of the band became rare at Cochiti, even though

Top: Fig. 55. KIUA POLYCHROME. *Ca. 1775–1900. Height 40.6 cm. Diameter 48.2 cm. Marjorie and Charles Benton Collection, Evanston, Ill. Many vessels of this period combined decorative features from a variety of sources. The rosette style and relatively light design suggest a Cochiti Pueblo origin for this jar. Rawhide lacing served both to stabilize the jar when filled and to facilitate handling.*

Bottom: Fig. 56. KIUA POLYCHROME (SANTO DOMINGO). *Ca. 1775–1925. Height 26.7 cm. Diameter 49.5 cm. Marjorie and Charles Benton Collection, Evanston, Ill. This bowl is characterized by extreme simplicity of design. A single band was divided into panels, which were filled in at the corners to form negative circles.*

FIGURE 56

FIGURE 58

KIUA POLYCHROME (SANTO DOMINGO). *Ca. 1775–1925. Height 25.4 cm. Diameter 26.7 cm. Marjorie and Charles Benton Collection, Evanston, Ill. The conservatism of Santo Domingo Pueblo was represented by long-term use of a simple, geometric design, as seen on this jar. One divergence was a ceremonial break, which is not shown.*

KIUA NEGATIVE POLYCHROME (SANTO DOMINGO). *Ca. 1900. Height 26 cm. Diameter 24.5 cm. The American Museum of Natural History, N.Y. 50.1 / 5030. Although the division of the design field on this jar is the same as other Kiua Polychromes, the black panels form a negative design. The use of the color red to balance the black was unusual.*

the framing lines persisted. Instead of formal geometrics, Cochiti Polychrome vessels had isolated figures illustrating natural phenomena such as clouds, rain, lightning, and birds. The framing lines sometimes carried appended arcs, triangles, or feathers. Elements were scattered and executed in relatively fine lines with small solids on a massive white or cream background. The drawings, however, were not done carefully.[39] Red was used only on the base of vessels.

Modeling had also become an important part of the Cochiti tradition. At first, appendages such as spouts modeled in the form of a head were placed on small, globular shapes. In the 1930s, potters began to make effigy vessels, human figures, fish, mountain sheep, and other shapes

that are made more realistic by painting the features. One woman, Terecita Romero, specialized in miniature polished black figures.[40] As mentioned earlier, a slightly different approach has been taken by Helen Cordero, who has become famous for her polychrome "Storyteller" figurines depicting an individual with many small children. Her other figures include "drummers" and "nativity figures." The increasing production of effigy vessels and figures at Cochiti has caused a decline in the production of jars and bowls.

Although the use of black carbon paint on a white or

56

FIGURE 59

FIGURE 60

Top:
Fig. 59. COCHITI POLYCHROME. *Ca. 1910–1920. Height 30.5 cm. Diameter 49.5 cm. Marjorie and Charles Benton Collection, Evanston, Ill. This jar is distinguished by the use of plant and cloud motifs that are more formally arranged than usual for many jars of this type.*

Bottom:
Fig. 60. COCHITI POLYCHROME. *Ca. 1900. Height 46.3 cm. Diameter 44.4 cm. Marjorie and Charles Benton Collection, Evanston, Ill. The motifs used in decorating the upper band of this jar were a carry-over from the Kiua style, but the design units and scattered elements are typical of Cochiti Polychrome. The use of red in the design was rare, usually found only on vessels made just before 1900.*

cream background at Santo Domingo and Cochiti was derived from Tewa polychromes to the north, Tewa design traditions were quite different after about 1750. In the Tewa pueblos, polychromes continued to be made, but styles deviated more and more from those described for Cochiti and Santo Domingo. At Tesuque, the earlier Powhoge Polychrome evolved into Tesuque Polychrome by 1875. Features that distinguish Tesuque Polychrome include meandering line motifs with appended curvilinear flourishes, stalked flowers, trident figures, pods, and a few life themes. The designs were confined to bands; on jars, the motifs used in the band around the neck contrasted with the band around the body. Red was used on the vessel base and only rarely appeared in the body motifs.[41]

Tatungue Polychrome, considered to have been a commercial form, began to be made in the late 1800s. The type was short-lived; it lasted only about forty years and was distinguished by the use of a faint blue and/or a red. Except for the blue and/or red additions, Tatungue Polychrome

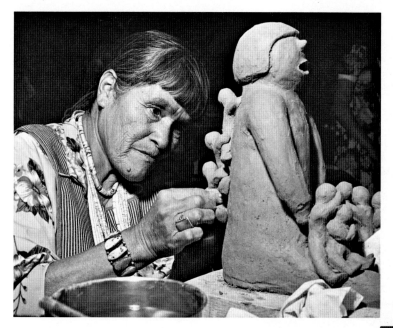

FIGURE 62

was similar in concept to Tesuque Polychrome; nevertheless, it appeared to be a model for the garish poster paint type that was introduced in the 1920s. Kenneth M. Chapman characterized it as "the Indian's idea of the White Man's idea of what Indian pottery should look like." Violent red, purple, blue, yellow, and white elements outlined with black, narrow lines were superimposed on a tan to brown background. This style has been facetiously referred to as Tesuque Anything-on-tan. The colors were applied after firing and smeared easily. Artistically, the pieces were poor, but many thousands of them entered the curio market and provided a much-needed income for that pueblo. Similarly, the so-called Tesuque "Rain-God" figures are often decorated with poster paint, and these too have found a good market as curios.

At Nambe, Tesuque's neighbor, potters stopped making polychromes by 1825 and began making a polished blackware. The type has been called Santa Clara Black, and the variety made at Nambe differed from that of Santa Clara only in the use of a softer paste that contained a large amount of mica. Slightly less mica and a harder paste were

58

characteristic of the Santa Clara Black produced at Pojoaque.[42] A few vessels continued to be made at Nambe until 1950, when the last potter died; none are identified from Pojoaque after about 1900.

The center for the best polished blackware, at least prior to 1920, was Santa Clara. Jar forms had an expanded body and high neck with scalloped rims, and in a few instances the neck was modeled after the twisted necks on blown glass vases. On bowls, the rim was scalloped also. A special form was the very large storage jar, which measured up to seventy-four centimeters high. One of the best-known hallmarks of Santa Clara Black made at Santa Clara was a repeated hand or "bear paw" imprint. The vessels showed an extremely high polish by 1930.[43]

Many aspects of the ceramic developments at Santa Clara after 1920 parallel those at San Ildefonso, especially in the matte black-on-burnished-black vessels. When these were not fired in a reducing atmosphere, the result was a matte red-on-burnished-red. Unique to Santa Clara were double-necked jars on which a strap handle bridges the two necks, often referred to as a "wedding jar." Innovations in

FIGURE 63

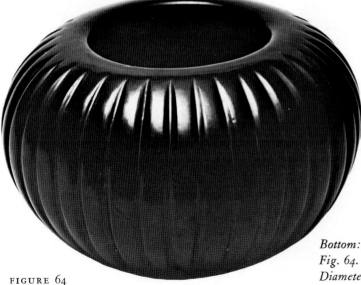

FIGURE 64

Top:
Fig. 63. SANTA CLARA BLACK, *Mela Youngblood. Ca. 1973. Height 43.2 cm. Diameter 25.4 cm. Marjorie and Charles Benton Collection, Evanston, Ill. The graceful body shape of this vase is a slightly modified version of those produced from the late 1800s to early 1900s. The stylized bear paw designs on the neck are characteristic of Santa Clara pottery.*

Bottom:
Fig. 64. SANTA CLARA BLACK, *Angela Baca. Ca. 1972. Height 15.2 cm. Diameter 24.1 cm. Marjorie and Charles Benton Collection, Evanston, Ill. The fluting of the surface on this globular jar has given rise to the term "squash jar" for vessels of this type.*

FIGURE 67

FIGURE 65

Top left:
Fig. 65. SANTA CLARA BLACK. *Ca. 1915. Height 23 cm. Diameter 19.5 cm. The American Museum of Natural History, N.Y. 50.1/3311. The "wedding vase" form of this vessel is characteristic of Santa Clara Pueblo. The body is highly polished, smudged, and fluted on this example.*

Bottom:
Fig. 66. SANTA CLARA CARVED BLACK, *Elizabeth Naranjo. 1975. Height 34.3 cm. Diameter 20.3 cm. Marjorie and Charles Benton Collection, Evanston, Ill. This jar has been carved to produce both relief and inset designs of feathers, stepped figures, and the Awanyu symbol.*

Top right:
Fig. 67. SANTA CLARA BLACK, *Virginia Ebelacker. 1975. Height 36.8 cm. Diameter 20.3 cm. Marjorie and Charles Benton Collection, Evanston, Ill. This highly polished "wedding vase" combines the characteristic double neck with the bear paw motif.*

FIGURE 66

decoration were seen in carved pieces on which positive motifs were created in bas-relief. The positive areas were given the same high polish as the body, but the depressed portions were matte painted.[44] Awanyu figures, stylized birds, and curvilinear or rectilinear scrolls were graceful in their simplicity.

The descendants of the Santa Clara potter Sarafina Tafoya, some thirty-nine of whom are involved in the art, have, in large part, manifested skill and creativity while adhering to traditional themes. Each has contributed new and imaginative variations. For example, Virginia Ebelacker makes carved and polished black vessels that, after firing, may be inset with turquoise and silver. Her son, Richard, specializes in making ceramic miniatures. Mary Ester Archuleta, who is married to a man from San Juan Pueblo, has combined the Santa Clara polished black with the San Juan Red incised techniques on the vessel. Camilio Sunflower Tafoya, Grace Medicine Flower, Joseph Lonewolf, and Rosemary Speckled Rock have developed a highly sophisticated form of ceramic art that is engraved before and after firing. Designs range from very simple petroglyph-like figures to entire scenes from pueblo life or mythology. Depending on the firing technique, the background might be red, black, or a resist area of the black smudged field.[45] Another treatment is one devised by Lela and Van Gutierrez of Santa Clara: light, almost-pastel greens, blues, and yellows are applied to a buff background, producing an earth tone effect that is atypical of Southwest design, although the elements and motifs remain Southwestern. Designs are intricate and show extreme attention to detail but at the same time have a flow that reduces tediousness. The Awanyu, or feathered and horned serpent, is a favorite representation. After Van died, Lela's son Luther decorated items made by either Lela or his sister, Margaret. Their work includes delightful animal figurines with almost laughing facial expressions. Stephanie Naranjo, Luther's granddaughter, is also involved in ceramics.[46]

Perhaps no other Rio Grande pueblo has received as much attention for its tradition of pottery-making as San

FIGURE 68

SANTA CLARA RED, *Margaret Tafoya. Ca. 1975. Height 38.1 cm. Diameter 33 cm. Marjorie and Charles Benton Collection, Evanston, Ill. This jar is distinguished by its form and polish. The artist has used the bear paw design as well as a narrow band applique.*

Ildefonso. What is unusual about the ceramic tradition there is the degree of recovery made after the craft almost died out between 1850 and 1880. Tourist trade after 1880 provided a new impetus, and San Ildefonso Polychrome came into existence to supply the demands of collectors. While the paste of this type was soft, it had a good, polished finish, and the painted decorations were well done. Red was again used in the designs, and the combinations became highly original. Birds, volute and curvilinear floral motifs, checkerboards, and even representations of the American

flag have been found. Almost all the containers were jars that were marked by a prominent bulge in the body, and the contracting neck was often either constricting or recurved. The banding that served to organize the decoration conformed to two distinct vessel areas. A white- to cream-colored slip was the background for black and red figures, while the base was slipped red. Identical motifs and vessel shapes were used in a red-slipped cognate type known as San Ildefonso Black-on-red.[47]

Tunyo Polychrome began to replace San Ildefonso Polychrome in the early 1900s, and it was the first ceramic style to be made by Maria Martinez, who is more commonly known simply as Maria. Tunyo Polychrome has been separated from the earlier types by attributes that include a return to a harder paste, thinner walls, and a change in the jar shape. While the prominent bulge of the body has been maintained, it becomes more convex, and the recurved neck approaches a height almost equal to that of the body. The white slip is somewhat streaky and no longer polished. Many of the motifs have been retained,

Left:

Fig. 69. SANTA CLARA CARVED RED, *Teresita Naranjo (Apple Blossom). Ca. 1974. Height 16.5 cm. Diameter 25.4 cm. Marjorie and Charles Benton Collection, Evanston, Ill. The use of a light cream color in the carved area on this jar heightens the contrast of the raised-relief bird-Awanyu design.*

Right:

Fig. 70. SANTA CLARA POLYCHROME, *Lela and Van Gutierrez. Ca. 1950s. Height 28 cm. Diameter 20.3 cm. Marjorie and Charles Benton Collection, Evanston, Ill. This vessel combines the traditional "wedding vase" form and the Awanyu figure with color combinations and design elements unique to the artists.*

FIGURE 71

SANTA CLARA POLYCHROME, *Margaret and Luther Gutierrez. Ca. 1974. Height 11.4 cm. Diameter 14.7 cm. Marjorie and Charles Benton Collection, Evanston, Ill. Almost unique design concepts have been used on this jar, making it a variety that is identified with the artists, more than with a traditional type.*

FIGURE 72

SAN ILDEFONSO POLYCHROME. *Ca. 1925. Height 43.2 cm. Diameter 56 cm. Marjorie and Charles Benton Collection, Evanston, Ill. After 1880, jars of this type were made in response to the tourist trade. Many combinations of highly original motifs came about as the result of the use of new symbols, such as the American flag, and red was used in the design.*

FIGURE 73

SAN ILDEFONSO BLACK-ON-RED. *Ca. 1900. Height 21.6 cm. Diameter 29.2 cm. Marjorie and Charles Benton Collection, Evanston, Ill. This type began to be made in the late 1800s, spanning the interval between San Ildefonso and Tunyo polychromes. The changes in its shape and design usually paralleled those of the polychromes.*

but each is somewhat larger and lacks appended elaborations. Bowls were produced again, and the interior often had a far more complex design than on jars.[48]

Maria and Julian Martinez began to experiment with black smudged pottery around 1917 after seeing the prehistoric materials recovered by Edgar L. Hewett from excavations on the Pajarito Plateau. Their own persistence, together with the encouragement received from Hewett and others, brought success by 1920. The new style was well received, and improvements continued to be stimulated by Kenneth M. Chapman, who purchased the best examples.[49] H. P. Mera was also important to the early ceramic advancements by San Ildefonso potters.

The acceptance of the black-on-black style led to a temporary disuse of light backgrounds and the abandonment of heavy motifs that had characterized Tunyo Polychrome.

Maria Martinez, San Ildefonso Pueblo, New Mexico. Best known for her rediscovery of the earlier blackware firing technology, Maria should also be credited with helping to establish the practice of signing Pueblo pottery in the 1920s.

FIGURE 75

FIGURE 76

Top left:
Fig. 75. SAN ILDEFONSO BLACK-ON-BLACK, *Maria Martinez and Popovi Da. Ca. 1955. Height 16.5 cm. Diameter 22.9 cm. Marjorie and Charles Benton Collection, Evanston, Ill. A matte paint was used on a highly polished background in order to produce the negative Awanyu figure that encircles this jar. When smudged, the polished surface created a contrast to the matte-paint area. The vessel was formed by Maria and painted by Popovi Da.*

Top right:
Fig. 76. SAN ILDEFONSO CREAM-ON-RED, *Maria Martinez and Popovi Da. Ca. 1955. Height 6.3 cm. Diameter 34.3 cm. Marjorie and Charles Benton Collection, Evanston, Ill. The artists employed the identical technique in producing this plate as in the one illustrated on page 66, except that it was not smudged in the firing process. A negative-style Awanyu figure with clouds has been used in the band design.*

Bottom:
Fig. 77. SAN ILDEFONSO SGRAFFITO, *Tony Da. 1968. Height 3.8 cm. Diameter 28 cm. Marjorie and Charles Benton Collection, Evanston, Ill. Using an engraved deer with a heartline inset with turquoise, the artist has succeeded in creating an abstract representation of a traditional motif, a style for which he is noted.*

FIGURE 77

FIGURE 78

Left:
Fig. 78. SAN ILDEFONSO BLACK-ON-BLACK, *Maria and Julian Martinez. Ca. 1935. Height 5.1 cm. Diameter 38.1 cm. Marjorie and Charles Benton Collection, Evanston, Ill. A radiating feather motif occupies the entire interior surface of this plate. The black-on-black decoration on vessels made today is the result of firing experiments by these two artists.*

Opposite page:
Fig. 79. TUNYO POLYCHROME, *Maria and Julian Martinez. Ca. 1920. Height 9.5 cm. Diameter 24.1 cm. Marjorie and Charles Benton Collection, Evanston, Ill. These artists began their ceramic efforts with polychromes of this style. They have used the Awanyu style motif on this bowl. The designs on bowls of this type are almost always more complicated than those on jars.*

The elements retained were modified to a simplified and more precisely executed style. The repetition of one or two motifs was much more common than the combination of many. Soon, the gracefulness of the vessel contours began to take precedence, and the flow of the muted paintings served to emphasize shape rather than call attention to combinations of color and content. A similar condition holds true for the unsmudged polished red pieces. When designs were carved on vessels, the same components were used; even on polychromes, the designs applied were characteristic of the black-on-black.

Maria and Julian disseminated what they had learned to members of their family and to others in the pueblo. Four of Maria's sisters as well as twelve other relatives have become skilled artists in their own right. Frequently, the craft has taken on a team approach, in which one individual constructs the vessel while another decorates it. Julian painted most of the early pieces made by Maria. Although their son, Popovi Da, was capable of both forming and painting, he decorated many of Maria's creations after the death of Julian. When Popovi Da died, his son, Tony Da, applied the designs on some of Maria's latest works. The skill of Tony Da can especially be seen in superb modeled and painted figures such as stylized bears, post-firing use of turquoise set into vessel walls, and use of a sgraffito engraving technique.[50] Some of the pieces that best reflect Maria's eagle feather motif are now made by Blue Corn.

Rosa Gonzales began her work with pottery around 1929 and is credited with being the first to make the carved style at San Ildefonso. Characteristically, her carving has rounded edges and a very high polish. Her son, Tse Pe, and his wife, Dora, have continued the craft. Dora is from Zia and was taught by her mother, Candelaria Gachupin. Not only have they worked in the carved style, but they have

FIGURE 79

FIGURE 80

FIGURE 81

FIGURE 82

Top left:

Fig. 80. SAN ILDEFONSO POLYCHROME, *Blue Corn. 1975. Height 15.2 cm. Diameter 15.2 cm. Marjorie and Charles Benton Collection, Evanston, Ill. The radiating feather motif that forms the band of decoration on the upper body of this jar is extremely simple but expertly conceived. The designs on this vessel may have been painted by the husband of the artist.*

Top right:

Fig. 81. SAN ILDEFONSO BLACK-ON-BLACK, *Blue Corn. Ca. 1965. Height 24.1 cm. Diameter 17.8 cm. Marjorie and Charles Benton Collection, Evanston, Ill. This vessel is similar in design to the one previously illustrated, but the black-on-black form of decoration was used.*

Bottom:

Fig. 82. SAN ILDEFONSO CARVED BLACK, *Rose Gonzales. Ca. 1974. Height 3.8 cm. Diameter 30.5 cm. Marjorie and Charles Benton Collection, Evanston, Ill. The artist has created an unusual heartline design with a bear paw motif in relief on this plate.*

FIGURE 83   FIGURE 84

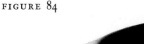

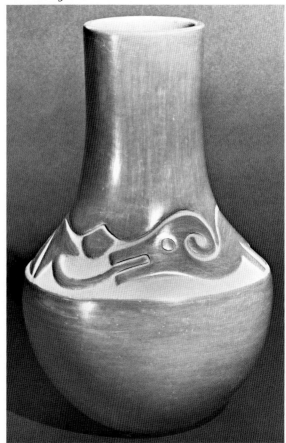

Left:

Fig. 83. SAN ILDEFONSO CARVED RED, *Rose Gonzales. Ca. 1960. Height 31.7 cm. Diameter 17.8 cm. Marjorie and Charles Benton Collection, Evanston, Ill. The differences between carved vessels produced at San Ildefonso and Santa Clara are difficult to distinguish. The Awanyu figure in relief on this vessel is not unlike Santa Clara examples.*

Right:

Fig. 84. BOWL, *Tse Pe and Dora, San Ildefonso Pueblo. 1974. Height 10.8 cm. Diameter 16 cm. Marjorie and Charles Benton Collection, Evanston, Ill. This vessel shows circular resist areas, which were created by placing a foreign object against the wall during the smudging.*

also made the black-on-black style and vessels decorated in a sgraffito manner with inset turquoise. Tse Pe and Dora have taught the craft to their four daughters.[51]

Ceramics from most of the post-Spanish period at San Juan Pueblo are poorly known. There are indications that several types inspired by the Spanish or by the Indians from Mexico who accompanied Oñate in 1598 were made at San Juan. One instance is a polished red with a glaze decoration: San Juan Glaze-on-red. What appears to be more typical of the early seventeenth century is a tan to buff body with a band of polished red slip below the rim. Known examples are referred to as San Juan Red-on-tan. They were probably made about 1750 to 1925. Many of the pieces entered the trade network, and some were carried by the Jicarilla Apache to settlements on the upper San Juan River between 1875 and 1925.

A ceramic revival occurred in the early 1930s as a result of efforts by an anonymous employee at the San Juan Day

FIGURE 85

Top:

Fig. 85. SAN ILDEFONSO BLACK-ON-BLACK, *Tonita and Juan. Ca. 1930. Height 45.7 cm. Diameter 45.7 cm. Marjorie and Charles Benton Collection, Evanston, Ill. Modeled after a storage jar, this vessel has dual bands of designs on the upper body. Feathers and stepped figures in panels are common to San Ildefonso pottery.*

Bottom:

Fig. 86. SAN JUAN RED-ON-TAN. *Ca. 1920. Height 28 cm. Diameter 44.4 cm. Fred Harvey Collection, The Heard Museum, Phoenix, Ariz. 595-P. The only modification of plainware on this vessel is its fine polishing and a band of red slip on the upper body. This style, probably introduced by the Spanish, has continued since the seventeenth century with only few changes in forms of vessels.*

Opposite page:

Fig. 87. SAN JUAN INCISED POLYCHROME, *Reyecita Trujillo. Ca. 1950. Height 30.5 cm. Diameter 30.5 cm. Museum of New Mexico Collections, Santa Fe. 18880/12. The old red-on-tan concept from San Juan Pueblo has been retained in the decoration of this vessel, but the artist has outlined complex bird and other motifs with incising. The spaces have been painted using white or a lighter red than the slip.*

FIGURE 86

School. With the encouragement of Kenneth M. Chapman, she set up art clubs, and the group selected Potsuwi'i Incised as the model for a new type.[52] Instead of retaining the gray of Potsuwi'i Incised, incising was adapted to the San Juan Red-on-tan, with the position of the colors reversed. The first pieces made were mostly bowls that had polished red lower walls and a tan upper segment, into which were incised shallow line decorations that utilized a Potsuwi'i style. Later, the incised lines became deeper and were filled with mica, especially on vessels with a uniform tan color. Regina Cata is the best-known potter identified with this revival. Luteria Atencio has also made both the incised as well as the older red-on-tan styles.[53]

San Juan has not confined itself to purely incised ware. Potters have also produced carved forms that sometimes

FIGURE 87

FIGURE 88

FIGURE 89

SAN JUAN RED-ON-TAN INCISED, *Felicita Garcia. Ca. 1972. Height 21.6 cm. Diameter 31.7 cm. Marjorie and Charles Benton Collection, Evanston, Ill. The ceramic revival of the 1930s at San Juan Pueblo brought about vessels that combined the earlier red-on-tan decoration with that of the older Potsuwi'i Incised, a style that is carried on today, as in this example.*

PICURIS MICACEOUS. *Ca. 1680 to present. Height 43.2 cm. Diameter 40.6 cm. The Heard Museum, Phoenix, Ariz. NA-SW-PS-A1-1. This large jar was probably made at Picuris Pueblo during the late 1800s. Its decorations were confined to fluting on both the applique and the rim. Scoring of the body copied Athapascan ceramic techniques.*

combine carving and incising. There is considerable difficulty in distinguishing the small carved pieces made at San Juan from those produced at Santa Clara and San Ildefonso. Still more recent is the filling of incised lines with red or the use of incised lines to outline painted areas of a polychrome. Motifs employed in polychromes run the gamut from simple geometrics to highly stylized birds, Awanyu elements, clouds, or kachina masks. The painted portion of globular jars has been confined to a wide band bounded by polished dark red areas on very short necks and bases. Colors include white and red on a matte tan background. Reyecita Trujillo is one potter active in producing the polychrome style.[54]

The ceramic tradition at the pueblos of Picuris and Taos will be characterized in chapter five (see page 108). After the Pueblo Rebellion of 1680, both locations adopted an Apachean style utilizing the local residual clay that became a golden color when fired properly. Form has been an overriding concern at Picuris and Taos, and many non-Indian items such as coffee pots, cream and sugar sets, and bean pots have been produced. While there is a certain beauty to their simple applique, scalloped rims, and color, utilitarian values have been more important than decorative concepts.

Now that we have outlined the diversity and trends found in recent ceramic art, in order to better understand these developments we will move from the present to the very beginnings of pottery-making and trace the history of the craft from its earliest forms.

Pueblo Pottery:
The Prehistoric Period

ARCHAEOLOGISTS HAVE DEFINED hundreds of types of pottery that were made by the Anasazi, the ancient occupants of the Pueblo region. To inspect each and every type in detail would be both tedious and not very enlightening. The prehistoric types that are considered here will be ones that illustrate the pattern and direction of prehistoric painted pottery. Perhaps the major compromise made here will be the brief treatment of plain and corrugated wares. These types, alone or in combination, generally constitute eighty to ninety percent of the sherds and vessels that have been recovered from Anasazi prehistoric sites.

In discussing prehistoric ceramics here, the major focus will be on wares, which are major technological groupings, as noted earlier. Often the distribution of a ware defines an area that archaeologists have identified as a discrete cultural area on other grounds. Sometimes, however, a large area may be characterized by a bewildering variety of wares. This latter case probably reflects a situation in which the Anasazi were importing pots, rather than producing them locally. In considering various wares, an effort will be made to identify some of the major cultural develop-ments with which particular stylistic patterns are associated.

As noted earlier, the first ceramics in the Puebloan world were recovered from sites that date to about the time of Christ. Elsewhere in the Southwest, the earliest ceramics were from sites occupied after 300 B.C. These remains were probably the product of occasional experimentation with ceramic manufacture, experimentation directly or indirectly reflecting the diffusion of an important technological tradition from Mesoamerica.

Pottery-making was not an independent invention of Southwestern peoples. Interaction with peoples to the south began indirectly by 2500 B.C., when primitive maize was first introduced to the Southwest. It was not until over 2,000 years later, however, that the production of ceramics followed. Once established, ceramic production in the southern Southwest continued to be influenced by style changes in the northern part of Mesoamerica, and these concepts were transmitted northward in a modified form.

The earliest ceramics found in the Puebloan area were brownwares, which occurred in contexts that appeared even earlier in the Mogollon area of Arizona and New Mexico.

Thus, there is an important question as to whether the early Anasazi potters were immigrants from the Mogollon region or simply influenced by the potters working in the south. Unfortunately, this question is not one that can be resolved at present. In fact, current study suggests a complex mixture of imported and locally manufactured brownwares.

In the Upper San Juan River Basin, for example, settled communities with houses of cribbed log construction were present between A.D. 1 and 400. The structures and accompanying artifacts bear strong resemblances to the remains of early Mogollon Tradition in southwestern New Mexico. In some of these excavated houses in the Upper San Juan River region, archaeologists have found plain brownware ceramics, including a poorly fired (or unfired) form of Los Pinos Brown as well as a fired form.[55] Plain brownware, Sambrito Brown, continued to be made through the period A.D. 400 to 700 with the development of sophisticated vessel forms. Surfaces were well polished but with no known painted decorations.[56] A plain brownware, Rosa Brown, continued to be made after black-on-white types came into use and may have represented persistence of the old technology for specialized small vessels, pipes, figurines, and whorls.[57] Early brownwares were also made in southern Utah and in the Little Colorado region, generally. As late as A.D. 550 to 950, ceramics in the Albuquerque area were brownware, suggesting continued movement of Mogollon peoples, ideas, or trade items into the area.

Obelisk Gray, A.D. 450 to 800, was the earliest ceramic type identified in central Arizona and is thought to be related to the Mogollon Tradition. In color, the paste ranged from a pale orange, through a light brown, to light or dark gray, and the surface exhibited a definite polish. Examples of the type with painted decorations have not been found.

The most widespread indigenous plainware type was Lino Gray, which was made by Anasazi potters at settlements throughout the area, beginning perhaps as early as A.D. 500. Lino Gray is a Tusayan Gray Ware, separated from other wares by a dark gray to almost black surface color and by larger, angular quartz temper particles that pierced the vessel surface, producing a sandpaper look. In the Mesa Verde area, Chapin Gray, which had crushed rock as well as sand temper, is a counterpart.

Brownwares were made by the Anasazi, as well as imported from the Mogollon. Graywares were certainly made by local artisans. That the brownwares led to local production of graywares is perhaps best indicated by experimentation found among transitional forms.

The period before A.D. 600, when plainwares were the almost exclusive product of local potters, was a time of low and very dispersed population. While there are indications of some villages that were larger than others and that may have been social, political, or economic centers, it is difficult to reach any firm conclusions concerning organizational patterns during this period. In much the same way, it would be problematical to attempt substantial interpretations of the ceramics. Fundamentally, this period was the first during which local peoples were experimenting with the production and distribution of ceramic products. To regard the epoch as other than experimental, to interpret distributional patterns as direct reflections of social and cultural processes, would be at least problematical and more probably erroneous.

In some Puebloan districts, plainware ceramics continued to be the most common ware right up into modern times. Unfortunately, we understand relatively little of the manner in which they were produced and distributed. These "utilitarian" wares have few distinctive characteristics for archaeologists to use in inferring relationships between pottery and social organization and behavior. The painted types that occurred along with plainwares during most of the Anasazi occupation of the Colorado Plateau allow for more specific inferences.

Corrugated pottery was made by leaving coils, or fillets, on the exterior surface of the pot. Designs were created both by the kinds of corrugation used and by the amount of a vessel covered. The surface of some corrugated types was covered by even, horizontal bands. Indentations varied considerably in width, height, and direction of overlap. Obliterated types were ones where a final scraping removed evidence of fillets. Incised and punched patterns occurred on some corrugated types. The alternation of different techniques of corrugation is called patterned corrugated.

Because of the bewildering variety of lines, shapes, depths, and patterns that were created in this fashion, corrugated wares are poorly understood. It is known that there were at least four major wares: a sand tempered brownware, a sand tempered grayware, a sherd tempered grayware, and a crushed-rock tempered brownware, but the design distinctions within these types are often poorly described at present.

Corrugated wares began to replace plainwares in most districts by A.D. 850–1000. In some areas of the Southwest, they completely replaced plainwares; in others, plainwares remained predominant; while in still others, there was a complex alternation through time. Later, corrugated wares were sometimes painted with one or more colors.

The Anasazi first began to produce painted pottery about A.D. 600, and Puebloan potters in some villages even today still make black-on-white vessels. While there was no time between A.D. 600 and the present when black-on-white types were not being produced somewhere in the Puebloan world, the heyday of black-on-white pottery-making was from about 850 to 1250.

A number of different changes were taking place among the Anasazi during these times. Above-ground pueblos were replacing pithouses, although not at precisely the same time in every district; some relatively large villages were built and occupied, villages of at least dozens and perhaps hundreds of rooms; some districts were heavily involved in agriculture, including the construction of extensive terracing and irrigation systems; and the population was much greater.

Had one been able to travel through the Anasazi area during this period, its most striking characteristic would probably have been diversity. The countryside would have been dotted with small farmsteads, and one would have occasionally passed small villages. The wooden structures and pithouses of the homesteads would have stood in strong contrast to the masonry pueblo villages. Staying in such a village for several days, one might have witnessed local members exchanging agricultural products and craft goods for hunted and gathered products with people from outlying areas. A complex mosaic of settlements and productive activities existed then, and ceramic distribution provides important clues to the manner in which local peoples organized their affairs.

Black-on-white pottery was never produced in great abundance. The vessels held by farmstead dweller and villager alike would have been predominantly plain or corrugated, depending on the time and the place. The average village dweller would probably have been in possession of a few painted pots, especially if these were viewed as having economic value or if they served as markers of social status.

While very little is currently known about the nature of ceramic production during this period, it is highly unlikely that every farmstead produced pottery and doubtful that even every village did. Essentially, this conclusion is reached because of the strong similarities in ceramic technology from particular parts of the Anasazi area.

Perhaps the most widely distributed black-on-white ware is Tusayan White Ware, which is distinguished from other wares by the use of temper composed of large, angular quartz sand particles and the use of carbon paint. Although its source is currently not known, such quartz sand might have been taken from deposits found in various districts of northeastern Arizona or, in this context, the area including the districts from the Little Colorado River north to the San Juan River in southeast Utah and from the Colorado River to the Chuska Mountains along the Arizona–New Mexico border.

The people of this region continued living in small pithouse villages up to the abandonment period. Larger villages typically consisted of several pithouses, a sub-surface kiva, and a surrounding arc of masonry surface storage rooms. Evidence of pottery-making in these villages is minimal, and preliminary petrographic studies suggest that it was probably being done in relatively few locations.

After about A.D. 1050, Tusayan White Ware was replaced by Little Colorado White Ware in the area between the

Hopi mesas and the Mogollon Rim on the north and south, and between Flagstaff and Holbrook on the west and east respectively. Little Colorado White Ware shared carbon paint with Tusayan White Ware, but had ground sherd rather than sand temper. Very little is known of sites in the Little Colorado area of this period. Generally, they seem to have been quite small, fifteen rooms constituting a large site. Kivas were found periodically and may have been ceremonial and political centers.

Little Colorado White Ware was a very short-lived phenomenon. A decline in production began by A.D. 1150, and few examples are found after 1250. Petrographic studies of this ware show a very substantial homogeneity of temper and paste characteristics across the entire region. Similarity of sherds from different areas is so great as to suggest only one or two centers of production.

The Mesa Verde region, in terms of the distribution of its distinctive ware, was an oval-shaped area extending through northwest New Mexico, southwest Colorado, and into southeast Utah. An approximate southern margin was the San Juan River, while the La Plata Mountains and the Dolores River in Colorado marked the northern limits. East to west, most of the ceramics were found between the Animas River of Colorado and the Abajo Mountains in Utah. Mesa Verde White Wares are distinguished from other wares by the use of crushed rock temper, especially andesite. Later, sherd temper was mixed with crushed rock. Paint type was variable, with carbon replacing mineral paint about A.D. 1150.

Today, the Mesa Verde area is one of the most accessible parts of the prehistoric Southwest. The extensive cliff dwellings are visited by millions of tourists each year. The area appears to have been one of the most densely populated in the Southwest in prehistoric times. As early as A.D. 850, large surface villages consisting of L-shaped blocks of rooms were in evidence. These grew in size and in distribution until they were eventually replaced by compact surface pueblos and extensive cliff dwellings. Little petrographic work has been done with Mesa Verde ceramics, but they were highly distinctive from other wares, and the standard-ization of design suggests at least some specialization in their production.

Ceramics that have been grouped together and called Cibola White Ware were manufactured over a large area from central-eastern Arizona eastward into the Rio Grande drainage of New Mexico. The segment of this region that lies in Arizona extends from the Mogollon Rim north to the Little Colorado–Rio Puerco (West) drainage and east of a north-south line near Joseph City, Arizona. In New Mexico, the region includes the Chaco Basin in the northwestern quarter of the state and, in the central-western section, through Ácoma and Zuñi as far south as the Mogollon Rim. It should be noted that the true extent of the region is far from clear, since there were periods when Cibola White Ware types were replaced by types from other wares, or when Cibola White Ware types were present outside this area.

There are a number of technological attributes that types of Cibola White Ware have in common. Mineral paint was used throughout in combination with a gray to white paste pottery. Temper in the early types was quartz sand, but after A.D. 875, crushed sherd was introduced and slowly replaced the sand. Because of this technological diversity, some scholars argue that the use of the term "ware" in the singular is incorrect — that, in fact, there are multiple Cibola White Wares, possibly from different production centers. The surfaces on the earliest types were poorly smoothed, and the temper protruded on the surface. Nevertheless, the technique of surface finishing improved rapidly, and after 950, most types were well polished at least on one surface and a thin to medium slip was applied. A high polish and a thick slip were characteristic between 1100 and 1250. After about 1300, glaze-paint decorated types, often polychrome, were favored, and Cibola White Ware died out. Even though the ware disappeared, many of the design concepts continued and later revivals drew upon them.

Tusayan, Little Colorado, Mesa Verde, and Cibola are four technological categories that represent the major productive distinctions during the period when the manufacture of black-on-white pottery predominated. Nevertheless, there were local exceptions of two sorts. First, archaeologists recognize minor differences in the percentage of tempering material or paint, which may reflect local manufacturing centers. Secondly, there were areas in which evidence of local production is minimal, such as the San Juan Basin and the Rio Grande area. In both areas, the majority of black-on-white types can be classified by comparing their technology to other areas. Nevertheless, there are occasional indications of local manufacture. In the case of the San Juan River region, local differences have been inferred on the basis of style. In the case of the Rio Grande, there are technological differences; of particular importance is the use of volcanic tuff temper for some types. While these are of minor quantitative importance, they suggest at least occasional local experimentation.

Certainly some aspects of variation among the wares reflect the increasing sophistication of the Anasazi artist. Formal treatment of the surface on the earliest vessels was minimal — the effort was simply to create the surface. Manipulation of the surface began with slipping, polishing, and corrugation. The most sophisticated examples of each of these treatments date to the period around A.D. 1300. Thus, the process of learning how to handle the surface underlies some of the variations described.

Clearly, many aspects of surface variation reflected local taste, and the changes in pigment types used through time provide a case in point. The earliest painted types in northern Arizona used carbon paint. Mineral pigments were typical in New Mexico and the Mesa Verde area, and by the late 1000s, carbon paint began to replace mineral paint among the pottery of Mesa Verde and the San Juan Basin. This change also took place in the Rio Grande Valley beginning about 1225. But during this same period, mineral paints were replacing carbon pigments in the portion of Arizona south of the Little Colorado River; in the Zuñi and Ácoma areas, mineral pigments were used throughout. Glaze paints appeared briefly about A.D. 700 but did not last. They were rediscovered or reintroduced about 1250 among craftspeople in east-central Arizona and spread eastward to

artisans in the Rio Grande Valley, where they lasted until about 1700.

Temper represents an intermediate aspect of variation. The widespread replacement of natural tempers by sherd tempers reflects the superiority of the latter; it had physical characteristics that produced somewhat stronger vessel walls. Nevertheless, variation in the use of the natural materials is clearly distinctive of localities, although crushed rock could have been used in many areas where sand predominated, and vice versa.

Because prehistoric potters clearly had options in regard to their use of pigments and temper, it is reasonable to infer that the wares reflected local manufacturing traditions. This is not to argue that the areas over which particular wares were distributed represented political or other social units. Rather, they were interactive zones in which prehistoric peoples probably maintained relatively stronger social, political, and economic ties. At least, they were areas in which the Anasazi exchanged common pieces of decorative art.

While variation in design is also specific to particular areas, major design traditions became widespread over the entire Anasazi area. The most basic of these styles were used in defining the pottery types of Tusayan White Ware. The earliest Tusayan style was Lino Black-on-gray. Since a type is a distinctive style within a ware, type names such as Lino Black-on-gray are also style names — that is, Lino style. Lino Black-on-gray design motifs were simple lines frequently ticked or fringed. There were often narrow bands framed by narrow lines, within which were rows of small dots. Solid elements were small and confined mainly to triangles on lines or filling in a corner at the junction of lines. This design concept is generally the style thought to be derived from basketry; motifs of Mogollon ceramic origin are less common.

Although Lino Black-on-gray appeared in dated contexts until A.D. 800, a number of innovations such as polishing and slipping on the interior of bowls and on the exterior of jars began to be used about 725. There was a corresponding change in style to Kana-a Black-on-white, on which the

FIGURE 90

FIGURE 91

designs are composed of contrasting elements. Groups of three or more fine parallel lines formed an angular band, with triangular solids filling the corners of the geometric spaces. The opposed edges of the triangles were usually ticked and cross-ticked lines, and they often divided the opposed units. Brushwork was casual, and the lines frequently extended beyond the point of intersection. Some solid pendant triangles had an extension of one side that ended in a hook.

The fine lines of Kana-a Black-on-white began to decrease about A.D. 855, when the wider line-work of Black Mesa Black-on-white became the preferred style. Included among the solid motifs were bands of positive or negative triangles, parallelograms, and diamonds. Parallel wide lines often became broadened in one section and evolved into interlocking curvilinear or rectilinear scrolls. Hatching was missing, but there was retention of ticking along the edges of some solids. An undecorated area in the bottom of the bowl was retained from the Kana-a Black-on-white pattern. The solid units were sometimes large enough to form negative motifs, which was a forecast of the later styles in the region.

The broad lines of Black Mesa Black-on-white continued to become still wider in Sosi style, which was made after A.D. 1075. The lines became uniform in width, however, and horizontal stripes made up a large part of the design. Almost all of the motifs were rectilinear, inter-

Top:
Fig. 90. KANA-A BLACK-ON-WHITE. *Ca.* A.D. *725–875. Height 16.5 cm. Diameter 13.5 cm. Arizona State Museum, University of Arizona, Tucson. GP–3466. Except for the use of carbon paint, the decorative motifs and patterning on this narrow-necked jar are identical with those on Kiatuthlanna Black-on-white.*

Bottom:
Fig. 91. BLACK MESA BLACK-ON-WHITE. *Ca.* A.D. *875–1130. Height 13.5 cm. Diameter 25.3 cm. Arizona State Museum, University of Arizona, Tucson. GP-1437. This bowl displays a mirrored design of solid elements that end in units with pendant dots, characteristic of its type. There are no panel divisions in the design.*

FIGURE 92

locked scrollwork. Solids included triangles and stepped elements that were distinct units rather than enlargements of the lines. There was also the beginning use of barbed lines, which continued later.

Dogoszhi style was a divergence from the solid line treatment, and it may have been copied from Cibola White Ware types. About A.D. 1085, artisans in various parts of the area began to experiment with hatching and the filling of bounded fields with parallel lines or squiggles. Hatching did not play an important role in subsequent black-on-white designs, however. The layout of the Dogoszhi style followed much the same pattern as the Sosi style; the distinction existed in wider elements that were filled with diagonal hatching. Framing lines and hatching lines were about the same width, even though both varied on a single piece of pottery. In only a few instances, solid lines divided the hatched elements. Some aspects of the concept were utilized on the later Polacca Black-on-white, but the hatching was bolder.

Potters producing Flagstaff Black-on-white used elements from the Sosi style, but with finer lines that were

Top:

Fig. 92. BLACK MESA BLACK-ON-WHITE. *Ca.* A.D. *875–1130. Height 45.7 cm. Diameter 40.6 cm. Field Museum of Natural History, Chicago, Ill. 21791. While wide lines with pendant solids replaced the contrasting fine lines of Kana-a Black-on-white, the pendant dots were retained on this particular type as an embellishment on solids or on the ends of scrolls.*

Bottom:

Fig. 93. SOSI BLACK-ON-WHITE. *Ca.* A.D. *1075–1200. Height 9.7 cm. Diameter 21.3 cm. The American Museum of Natural History, N.Y. 29.1/2257. The dominant attributes of this bowl are solid, carbon paint lines, more heavily drawn than on Black Mesa Black-on-white. The pendant dots found on the latter have been replaced by stepped elements, in a three-fold repetition of the motifs.*

FIGURE 93

79

FIGURE 94   FIGURE 95

FIGURE 96

Top left:
Fig. 94. DOGOSZHI BLACK-ON-WHITE. *Ca.* A.D. *1085–1200. Height 21.6 cm. Diameter 15.2 cm. School of American Research Collections in the Museum of New Mexico, Santa Fe. 8419/11. This pitcher displays a band of simple triangular figures filled with horizontal parallel lines. Like Puerco Black-on-white pitchers, the transition from the body contour to the neck is a smooth curve.*

Top right:
Fig. 95. FLAGSTAFF BLACK-ON-WHITE. *Ca.* A.D. *1100–1200. Height 6.5 cm. Diameter 13.5 cm. Arizona State Museum, University of Arizona, Tucson. GP-9175. On this bowl, a four-fold repetition of the motif is dominated by typical opposed saw-tooth elements. The closely spaced elements and negative scrolls near the rim indicate a trend toward negative designs.*

Bottom:
Fig. 96. KAYENTA BLACK-ON-WHITE. *Ca.* A.D. *1250–1300. Height 11 cm. Diameter 21.3 cm. The American Museum of Natural History, N.Y. 29.1/4801. The negative decorative style on this bowl was created by crosshatching the large element and then painting all but selected squares. The amount of white background was further reduced by placing dots in the squares. This motif has a textile quality.*

FIGURE 97

FIGURE 98

often barbed and that occurred in opposed pairs. While the style was not a negative paint style, a much heavier percentage of the vessel surface was covered with black paint. Some spaces were filled with diagonal hatchings or crosshatchings, and when squares were formed, they often contained a small dot. Small solid triangles with interlocking hooks were arranged in bands, especially on the flared rims of bowls. Except when open spaces were left in the bottom of a bowl, the amount of painted area was approximately equal to the unpainted background.

Beginning in the mid-1100s, some potters used negative paint styles, in which black paint was applied so heavily that it formed the background and white slip formed the design. This is referred to as Kayenta style, although it occurs on other black-on-white types. In the Black-on-white types, Wupatki and Betatakin, an open-work effect was created by crosshatching to form a grid, a portion of which was filled in much the same way as one would fill squares on graph paper. The grid areas were usually bounded by heavy lines or bands of solid triangles. By A.D. 1200, massed solids were becoming more common, and on some types there were negative curvilinear or rectilinear scrolls, stepped

Left:
Fig. 97. BETATAKIN BLACK-ON-WHITE. *Ca.* A.D. *1150–1300. Height 8.2 cm. Diameter 18.4 cm. Marjorie and Charles Benton Collection, Evanston, Ill. The layout of the design on this bowl is nearly identical to Figure 96, on page 80. An earlier date of production is suggested by the slightly more open appearance, less polish, and the lack of a rim decoration.*

Right:
Fig. 98. TUSAYAN BLACK-ON-WHITE. *Ca.* A.D. *1150–1300. Height 40.6 cm. Diameter 38.1 cm. Field Museum of Natural History, Chicago, Ill. 75101. The negative style characteristic of this type is shown on this jar decorated with closely spaced elements. Often, the spaces between the interlocked scrolls were painted solid black.*

lines dividing solid areas, or a fine negative grid resembling embroidery. After 1300, except for Bidahochi Black-on-white, all other black-on-white pottery types disappear from the region of northeastern Arizona.

A group of types related to Tusayan White Ware occurred in the Upper San Juan River region. Rosa Black-on-white, the earliest within the group, A.D. 700–900, exhibited

FIGURE 99

FIGURE 100

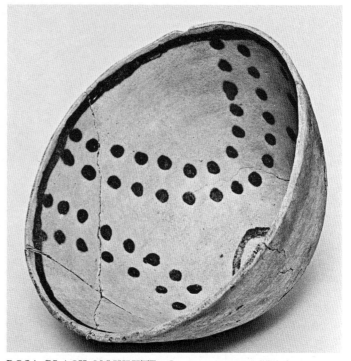

BIDAHOCHI BLACK-ON-WHITE. *Ca.* A.D. *1300–1400. Height 13 cm. Diameter 14 cm. Arizona State Museum, University of Arizona, Tucson. GP-8981. Decorations on this pitcher illustrate a movement away from the negative style of Kayenta Black-on-white. The alternating crosshatched panels were not filled in, and the linework is less exacting.*

ROSA BLACK-ON-WHITE. *Ca.* A.D. *700–900. Height 11.4 cm. Diameter 16.5 cm. Museum of New Mexico Collections, Santa Fe. 43660/11. This open, hemispherical bowl has carbon paint decorations confined to the interior surface. A heavy line separates the festoon alignments of parallel dots.*

ARBOLES BLACK-ON-WHITE. *Ca.* A.D. *950–1050. Height 7.6 cm. Diameter 19.4 cm. Museum of New Mexico Collections, Santa Fe. 44284/11. This bowl is representative of the type in the use of opposed motifs from a rim band line. The cross-ticked lines in the triangles and the solid saw-tooth elements were retained from the earlier Piedra Black-on-white.*

FIGURE 101

FIGURE 102

GALLINA BLACK-ON-WHITE. *Ca.* A.D. *950–1300. Height 9 cm. Diameter 17.1 cm. School of American Research Collections in the Museum of New Mexico, Santa Fe. 8460/11. The designs on this bowl are dominated by unbalanced and asymmetrical line-filled areas. The simple circle bounded by concentric arcs in the bottom of the bowl was an early motif in the Southwest.*

FIGURE 103

LA PLATA BLACK-ON-WHITE. *Ca.* A.D. *600–800. Height 11.2 cm. Diameter 16.5 cm. The American Museum of Natural History, N.Y. H/11138. This deep bowl resembles coiled basketry in both its shape and the simplicity of its design. It was probably made in western New Mexico and reached the Rio Grande as a result of trade.*

designs built up from a circle at the bottom of a bowl or, on a jar form, used the opening as a point of departure from which design symmetry was constructed. Line-work was far more common than solid figures, and independent motifs, often in the form of concentric circles, were sometimes bounded by lines with pendant solid triangles.

By A.D. 850, Piedra Black-on-white began to characterize pottery in the upper reaches of the San Juan River. The examples of this type found in the Upper San Juan River region exhibited few divergences. Mineral paint was used, and there was an emphasis on designs made of groups of narrow parallel lines often arranged in a zigzag pattern. It is important to note that the appearance and development of the Piedra style became the basis for many of the later designs in the Upper San Juan River region.

The local successor to Piedra Black-on-white was Arboles Black-on-white, which spanned the period from A.D. 950 to 1050. Designs were almost entirely limited to a bold treatment of the Piedra style, but the quality of draftsmanship declined. Examples of the Sosi and Dogoszhi styles here were rare.

The other ceramic development out of Rosa Black-on-white occurred largely in the southeastern part of the region, and it was much more conservative. Carbon paint was used, and designs were derived from a Rosa-Piedra style. The transition type to the later Gallina Black-on-white has been termed Bancos Black-on-white, which dated approximately between A.D. 850 and 1000.

FIGURE 104

Top:

Fig. 104. ESCAVADA BLACK-ON-WHITE. *Ca.* A.D. *925–1125. Height 18 cm. Diameter 15.5 cm. The American Museum of Natural History, N.Y. H-3585. The major distinction separating this variety from others of the Puerco Black-on-white style is the dominance of wide line elements in the design. (See appendix, p. 143)*

Bottom:

Fig. 105. GALLUP BLACK-ON-WHITE. *Ca.* A.D. *950–1100. Height 28 cm. Diameter 31.8 cm. Marjorie and Charles Benton Collection, Evanston, Ill. On this vessel, the motifs of hatched geometric scroll figures have been alternated in the band and contrast with the checkerboard design of the neck. The use of this motif was characteristic of this variety of Puerco Black-on-white.*

Opposite page, left:

Fig. 106. PUERCO BLACK-ON-WHITE. *Ca.* A.D. *950–1100. Height 45.7 cm. Diameter 37.5 cm. Arizona State Museum, University of Arizona, Tucson. GP-2134. The transition from the body to the neck of this pitcher is a smooth curve, rather than a sharp angle as found in several other types of this period. The repetition of the same designs in both the upper and lower bands is another unusual feature, but the vertical lines that divide the bands into panels are characteristic.*

Opposite page, right:

Fig. 107. CHACO BLACK-ON-WHITE. *Ca.* A.D. *1050–1125. Height 16.5 cm. Diameter 10 cm. The American Museum of Natural History, N.Y. H/3277. Pitchers of this type are characterized by their cylindrical neck and small expanding bodies. The junction of the neck and body is marked by a sharp corner.*

(See appendix, p. 143)

FIGURE 105

FIGURE 106

FIGURE 107

Major stylistic patterns contrasting with Tusayan styles were those of the Cibola White Wares. Nevertheless, early Cibola types are similar to Tusayan wares in their style. La Plata Black-on-white, except for its mineral paint, is identical to Lino Black-on-gray and was made beginning about A.D. 600. White Mound Black-on-white, Kiatuthlanna Black-on-white, and Red Mesa Black-on-white drew basically on Kana-a and Black Mesa styles, along with some elements of design from the Mesa Verde area. These styles were common between about 700 and 950.

At about this time, the first distinctive Cibola styles were made. From the Rio Puerco (West) and Rio San Jose northward into the Chaco Basin, the dominant type was Puerco

Black-on-white, which is divided into three styles: Escavada, Gallup, and Puerco.[58] The Escavada style has been characterized by heavy line-work with solid triangles, interlocking scrolls, and checkerboards. Elements were often combined with sets of crudely drawn, heavy parallel lines, or with a band of angled hatching enclosed by lines somewhat heavier than the hatching.[59] The Gallup style, on the other hand, had a predominance of somewhat finer hatched elements. The designs were so arranged that the background forms a part of the pattern. Often, the hatched figures were scrolls, either used alone or interlocked.[60] Heavy

FIGURE 108

FIGURE 109

lines and lines with pendant solid triangles often occurred between the motifs, but they were rarely used in the form of an opposed arrangement. The Puerco style departed from the two previous ones in having designs arranged in bands that often were divided into panels by a series of parallel vertical lines. The units created contained opposed solids, rectilinear scroll figures ending in keys, or checkerboards. On some examples, the band consisted of vertical parallel lines alternating with horizontal parallel lines.[61]

Chaco Black-on-white — which is generally, though not absolutely, Dogoszhi style — is thought to be derived from the Gallup variety of Puerco Black-on-white. The symmetry pattern of Chaco Black-on-white was a departure from the previous Gallup style.[62] It is quite probable that Chaco Black-on-white was produced by specialists in a complex society. The large sites such as Pueblo Bonito and Chetro Ketl in Chaco Canyon were probably trading centers at this time. Many exotic goods have been recovered through excavations, and there are constructed prehistoric roads leading in several directions from Chaco Canyon.

Reserve Black-on-white was made between A.D. 950 and 1100 in central-eastern Arizona and adjacent parts of New Mexico along the Mogollon Rim and immediately south into the mountain belt. Reserve style used a number of new design elements — for example, diagonal hatching, stepped elements, fine narrow lines, and the use of a band decora-

Top:
Fig. 108. RESERVE BLACK-ON-WHITE. *Ca.* A.D. *950–1100. Height 15 cm. Diameter 15 cm. Arizona State Museum, University of Arizona, Tucson, GP-3127. Although this style was carried on into Tularosa Black-on-white, the open design and relatively uniform width of lines distinguished it from later developments.*

Bottom:
Fig. 109. TULAROSA BLACK-ON-WHITE. *Ca.* A.D. *1100–1250. Height 30.5 cm. Diameter 36.8 cm. Marjorie and Charles Benton Collection, Evanston, Ill. The intricate band pattern on this large jar was formed by a complex meshing of two registers: an upper one of rectangular opposed scrolls and a lower one of curvilinear scrolls. In contrast to the earlier Reserve Black-on-white, the elements are closer together, solids are heavier, and the hatching lines are finer.*

FIGURE 110

FIGURE 111

tion rather than an all-over layout. Opposed hatched and solid elements in a Wingate style, and solids similar to Sosi or Puerco style, were most frequently used.[63]

Reserve evolved into the Tularosa style, made from 1100 to 1250. Dominant differences were a more highly polished, thick white slip; a greater use of longitudinal hatching that was finer and closer spaced; heavier framing lines bounding the hatched elements; and the use of smaller and more compact solid elements. There was a progressively greater amount of the background covered, until a negative style was approached in the late pieces. Although these differences occur in treatment, the basic style was little changed from the earliest examples.[64] A somewhat greater emphasis on the use of solids seems to have taken place in vessels produced in the north, and Tularosa Black-on-white appears to last slightly longer there.

Despite these distinctive styles, there were also Cibola styles that continued to parallel Tusayan styles. Snowflake Black-on-white is a Sosi style based on Cibola technology.[65] Unfortunately, Snowflake has also been used as a catchall category for the more esoteric designs found in the area, and hence its delineation is difficult.

In addition to the influence of Mogollon brownware types, early Anasazi ceramics in the Rio Grande region included the non-decorated Lino Gray, Lino Fugitive Red, Kana-a Gray, and the beginnings of local forms with micaceous and schist inclusions. Most of the decorated types

Top:
Fig. 110. ROOSEVELT BLACK-ON-WHITE. *Ca.* A.D. *1250–1300. Height 20 cm. Diameter 88 cm. Arizona State Museum, University of Arizona, Tucson. GP-8240. This type is considered to be a regional development similar to Tularosa Black-on-white, but it is distinguished by decorative styles that suggest adaptations from late Hohokam ceramic traditions. It is a southern Anasazi development.*

Bottom:
Fig. 111. SNOWFLAKE BLACK-ON-WHITE. *Ca.* A.D. *950–1200. Height 9.5 cm. Diameter 20.5 cm. The Heard Museum, Phoenix, Ariz. NA-SW-AZ-A2-267. The band design on this bowl was executed in a Sosi style, with wide-lined interlocking scrolls that terminate in stepped elements. The ticking on the rim was not common.*

FIGURE 112   FIGURE 113

SNOWFLAKE BLACK-ON-WHITE: *Ca.* A.D. *950–1200. Height 19.1 cm. Diameter 20.3 cm. Marjorie and Charles Benton Collection, Evanston, Ill. Although this type incorporated many design styles, the motifs by which it has been defined are interlocked and opposed stepped solids. On many examples, the black mineral paint was glossy and almost a sub-glaze.*

RED MESA BLACK-ON-WHITE. *Ca.* A.D. *900–1100, in the Rio Grande region. Height 7 cm. Diameter 17.9 cm. Marjorie and Charles Benton Collection, Evanston, Ill. The motifs on this bowl are more simplified and bolder than those produced west of the Rio Grande region. The horizontal handles and the use of corrugation are unusual.*

appear to have been imported, and among these were Lino Black-on-gray, the Black-on-white types of La Plata, White Mound, Kiatuthlanna, Red Mesa, and an unnamed variety of Red Mesa Black-on-white. Two types considered to be local were San Marcial Black-on-white and another unnamed variety of Red Mesa Black-on-white. Both were essentially Cibola White Wares, and, as with all those types, mineral paint was used. San Marcial Black-on-white might have been a variety of the western White Mound Black-on-white but was characterized by a smoother surface and mineral paint that was almost always oxidized to a reddish brown.

The local variety of Red Mesa Black-on-white, which lasted through most of the A.D. 1000s, differed from the form west of the Rio Grande Valley by the use of a local paste

and slightly bolder decorative elements. Surface treatment displayed a thin slip that became a hallmark of the subsequent local types, Kwahe'e Black-on-white and Taos Black-on-white, which appeared in the late 1000s. The impetus for the development of these two types may have been the movement of groups from the northern part of the Upper San Juan River Basin into parts of the northern Rio Grande Valley.

Contemporaneous with the development of the two Black-on-white types, Kwahe'e and Taos, Socorro Black-on-white spread into the Rio Grande Valley from the west. The first two types were primarily found north of Albuquerque, but the latter occurred characteristically to the south, extending into the region of brownwares south of Socorro, New Mexico. This division of the northern Rio Grande Valley remained, to a general extent, into the Historic period; a later glaze-decorated ware appeared in the district where Socorro Black-on-white was found, and

FIGURE 114   FIGURE 115

CHUPADERO BLACK-ON-WHITE. *Ca.* A.D. *1150–1400 or later. Height 25 cm. Diameter 25 cm. The Heard Museum, Phoenix, Ariz. NA-SW-AZ-A2-215. This type retained many of the design attributes from its predecessor, Socorro Black-on-white.*

SOCORRO BLACK-ON-WHITE. *Ca.* A.D. *950–1400. Height 30.5 cm. Diameter 30.5 cm. School of American Research Collections in the Museum of New Mexico, Santa Fe. 8182/11. This was a long-lived type for which there were temporal distinctions based on subtle changes in design. The example here was probably produced between* A.D. *1100 and 1200. Opposed hatched and solid geometric elements were characteristic, but, as shown, the opposed units were not always identical.*

later carbon paint ceramics replaced the Kwahe'e and Taos Black-on-white types.

Most studies of Socorro Black-on-white designs have concentrated on temporal changes. The two recognized regional variations are Chupadero Black-on-white and Casa Colorado Black-on-white. Both were found south and southeast of the area where Socorro Black-on-white occurred, and Chupadero Black-on-white eventually spread over much of southeastern New Mexico.

The last local ceramic development of the Prehistoric period, Santa Fe Black-on-white, began in the district north of Albuquerque about A.D. 1225. Most of the earlier Taos and Kwahe'e motifs were present but now covered more of the background within the band area. Although the designs appeared to evolve from local ideas, the shift to carbon paint may have been a concept derived from Mesa-Verde-inspired ceramics found on the western margin of the Rio Grande region at this time.

The design styles on Little Colorado White Ware directly paralleled those on Tusayan White Ware. It was not until A.D. 1050, however, that sherd tempered types became common. Thus, no pottery comparable to Lino Black-on-gray was sherd-tempered. The type equivalent to Kana-a Black-on-white in the Little Colorado White Ware tradition is said to be St. Joseph Black-on-white, although only

FIGURE 116

FIGURE 117

SANTA FE BLACK-ON-WHITE. *Ca.* A.D. *1225–1350. Height 11.4 cm. Diameter 13 cm. Museum of New Mexico Collections, Santa Fe. 43676/11. This type was the first of the carbon-paint decorated ceramics made in the Rio Grande region and is considered to be the incipient form from which the long list of Tewa-style ceramics developed. The decorations on this small jar with mushroom-shaped lug handles consist of opposed solid and hatched figures that are arranged in panels.*

WALNUT BLACK-ON-WHITE. *Ca.* A.D. *1100–1125. Height 43.2 cm. Diameter 43.2 cm. Marjorie and Charles Benton Collection, Evanston, Ill. This large jar is a superior example of the type. The layout of the design may have been inspired by the weave of a textile.*

a handful of sherds has been found. Only the later examples of Black Mesa Black-on-white had a sherd-tempered decorated counterpart, Holbrook Black-on-white. There were varieties of both Holbrook Black-on-white and late Black Mesa Black-on-white that differed only in the use of an indented corrugated exterior. Sosi style of Little Colorado technology is called Holbrook B, to be distinguished from Holbrook A for Black Mesa; Padre Black-on-white is the Little Colorado equivalent of Dogoszhi Black-on-white; and Walnut Black-on-white is the equivalent of Flagstaff Black-on-white.

Mesa Verde White Ware styles represented a contrast-

ing pattern to the style above. While in a basic sense they reflected the Tusayan and Cibola styles, distinctive local elements were almost always added. Chapin Black-on-white, made between A.D. 600 and 900, was in most respects an equivalent of Lino Black-on-gray. As with Lino style, the design was open and built up from the bottom in a basket-like fashion. Added elements included triangles, short dashes or ticks, dots, hooks, and combinations of these. Fillers between parallel lines consisted of dots; cross figures; short, slanted lines; and stepped elements. Motifs also occurred isolated in the field but opposed to others of similar form.

Piedra Black-on-white, made between A.D. 750 and 900, had a style that was basically that of Kana-a Black-on-white

FIGURE 118

CHAPIN BLACK-ON-WHITE. *Ca.* A.D. *575 or 600–875. Height 9.5 cm. Diameter 14 cm. Arizona State Museum, University of Arizona, Tucson. GP-46407. Decorative styles of this type reflect the concepts found widely among most early black-on-white types, but this piece is distinguished from the others by the inclusion of crushed rock temper.*

FIGURE 119

PIEDRA BLACK-ON-WHITE. *Ca.* A.D. *850–950. Height 11 cm. Diameter 18.3 cm. The American Museum of Natural History, N.Y. 29.1/3259. This bowl shows the trend toward a shallower but still open form. The design, drawn with mineral paint, consists of three spaced motifs of an outlined cross with appended key shapes. A small circle in the bottom of the bowl is partially visible. Representatives of this type were made in the Mesa Verde region as early as* A.D. *750, but were not common in the Upper San Juan River region until 850.*

but different in many of the same respects that Chapin Black-on-white differed from Lino Black-on-gray. In addition, there were independent motifs, usually centered at the bottom of bowls and often consisting of a crossed element outlined with one or more lines of approximately the same width.[66]

Cortez Black-on-white, made from A.D. 900 to 1000, was basically Black Mesa style with Mesa Verde additions. Mancos Black-on-white, made between 950 and 1150, included both Sosi and Dogoszhi art styles with the typical Mesa Verde additions. The latest Mesa Verde types were, stylistically, the most distinctive.

McElmo Black-on-white and Mesa Verde Black-on-white were carbon paint types, and both have been found in sites as far south as the Canyon de Chelly district and Chaco Basin. McElmo Black-on-white, made from 1075 to 1275, resembled the previous Mancos Black-on-white in design, but the hatching lines were slightly heavier and there were combinations of narrow and broad lines. De-

signs often occurred in a band on the interior of bowls and exterior of jars; bands were bounded by framing lines and were sometimes divided into panels. Within the panels, opposed hatched and solid elements were present.[67]

Better craftsmanship characterized the evolution of the designs into those of Mesa Verde Black-on-white, made between A.D. 1200 and 1300. The motifs were more closely spaced, and the amount of painted area was about equivalent to the amount of background. Contrasts between lines and solids, or between hatched figures and solids, were frequent. There was an emphasis on building the designs by a process of dividing and subdividing the decorative field

FIGURE 120

McELMO BLACK-ON-WHITE. *Ca.* A.D. *1075–1275. Height 8.2 cm. Diameter 17.1 cm. Marjorie and Charles Benton Collection, Evanston, Ill. The simple band organization of the design on this bowl has been divided into alternate equivalent panels. Decorations on the rim consist of ticking and correspond to the checkerboard motif. The design on this vessel is much less complex than those of later Mesa Verde Black-on-white examples.*

FIGURE 121

MESA VERDE BLACK-ON-WHITE. *Ca.* A.D. *1200–1300. Height 15.5 cm. Diameter 32.3 cm. The American Museum of Natural History, N.Y. 29.1/2189. The latest ceramics in the Mesa Verde region had an intense and formal design. Here, a band layout on the bowl interior contains crowded motifs of opposed but unequal solid and hatched elements.*

into progressively smaller units, with subsequent filling in of certain spaces. Almost all designs were well organized and symmetrical; they were abstract and geometric except for an occasional stylized biomorphic figure, which occurred either on the bowl exterior or in the center of the interior.[68]

A variety of Mesa Verde Black-on-white, Mesa Verde Polychrome, utilized a combination of paints. The designs remained the same, but a black mineral paint was used to outline solid figures, and the interior of the figure was filled with a thin, organic paint that provided contrast.[69]

At any one time period, ceramics from the Anasazi area were far less varied in their style than in their technology, suggesting a substantial, although not highly organized, amount of communication over the entire Colorado Plateau. When similar styles were painted on quite differently made pots using chemically different pigments, the conclusion that there was relatively direct and substantial contact or communication among artisans seems obvious. At the same time, there were enough differences in the interpretation and execution of particular styles to preclude the notion that they were produced by one specialist or even a few.

In most respects, stylistic variation seems to reflect variation in artistic tastes through time. Nevertheless, there are obvious spatial boundaries to the styles we have discussed thus far. Tusayan styles predominated to the north and west, Cibola styles to the south and east. Whether these represented real organizational boundaries or simply arbitrary limits of "taste" cannot be determined at present. It is interesting, nevertheless, that many of the northeastern styles never penetrated southwestern areas, and vice versa. Perhaps the eastern versus western organizational patterns seen among modern Pueblo villages had prehistoric, although spatially somewhat different, roots.

At the same time, it is important to realize that there were many areas of the Colorado Plateau that cannot easily be defined in respect to either the technological or stylistic categories that have been considered so far. They were the tension zones between the major traditions. One enclave that seemed to maintain a somewhat distinctive tradition throughout most of the Prehistoric period lay along the upper Rio San José.

Local ceramic types produced there paralleled those of the Cibola White Ware. Minor differences existed in surface finish, ratio of bowl to jar forms, and the frequent use of a lustrous black paint instead of the usual matte black. Bluewater Black-on-gray was the unslipped equivalent of Red Mesa Black-on-white; Las Tusas Black-on-gray (unslipped) and Grants Black-on-white (slipped) were similar to the Escavada variety of Puerco Black-on-white; and San Mateo Black-on-gray (unslipped) and Prewitt Black-on-white (slipped) were more like the Gallup variety.[70] At this time, these types are more useful in an analytical sense than in the broader perspective of design development, but they do illustrate the individualism expressed during the Prehistoric period.

While black-on-white wares were predominant during the periods under discussion, vessels with black paint on red to yellow surfaces were also made. These types (bichromes) might represent the continuation of a Mogollon-like tradition within the area, but their relationships to black-on-white styles suggest an occasional center in which particular design traditions were applied to a different paste.

The period during which bichromes other than black-on-white types were made remains indefinite. It is clear that such types were made early in Anasazi prehistory and that they continued to be manufactured beyond the time when black-on-white types were characteristic; at the present time, however, there are not enough well-excavated sites to suggest any clear boundary to their production. In a fundamental sense, bichromes seem to represent a transitional form between black-on-white and polychrome types.

The earliest bichromes were the redware types of the lower San Juan region. Although these pieces were traded over an area much larger than the northeast Arizona region, the centers from which they spread appear to have been in the northern part of the region. The red background remained popular throughout most of the Prehistoric period, but between A.D. 1050 and 1300 there was a proliferation of types with a paste that fired orange, and

FIGURE 122

94

only a few such types remained after 1400. Beginning about 1275, however, they were replaced with a decorated pottery made from a clay that fired yellow, and this yellow background became the model for most decorated pottery up to the present day.

The essential relationship between black-on-red and black-on-white types is best illustrated by the San Juan Red Ware types that shared styles with the Mesa Verde region. Abajo Red-on-orange, for example, incorporated both the basketry designs described on Chapin Black-on-white and Piedra Black-on-white, as well as styles reminiscent of Mogollon pottery of the same period in southeastern Arizona. The design field was divided bilaterally, quadrilaterally, by a spiral, banded, and with an overall design. Elements included broad parallel or wavy lines across, around, or in spirals from the base to the rim. Solid triangles arranged in rows, terrace or half-terrace figures, checkerboards, and concentric circles were common motifs. The line-work was generally poor, even though there was good balance.[71] Abajo Polychrome displayed the same designs but with the additional use of black paint along with the characteristic red.

Designs on Bluff Black-on-red departed in several respects from those on the earlier Abajo Red-on-orange and were unusual in terms of the expected direction based on other series. Symmetry patterns became much simpler, even though good balance was maintained. Much less of the background was covered by the design than on the earlier Abajo type. Lines were much better executed, however, and both wide and narrow lines sometimes appeared in

a design. Patterns remained geometric, even for the biomorphic motifs. Most patterns were pendant from the rim, in contrast with the patterns on many black-on-white types of the same period that were built up from the bottom of the bowl.[72]

Deadmans Black-on-red, including La Plata Black-on-red as a regional variety, emphasized groups of equal width parallel lines, usually in a zigzag pattern.[73] Small solid triangles often filled the angles left by a directional change

FIGURE 123

ABAJO RED-ON-ORANGE. *Ca.* A.D. *700–850. Height 10.2 cm. Diameter 23.5 cm. Museum of New Mexico Collections, Santa Fe. 43928/11. The use of specular iron paint or a mixture of red iron oxide, magnetite, and quartz to create the nested triangles and parallel lines with saw-tooth solids was uncommon in the Southwest; the decoration is reminiscent of vessels found in the Mogollon region.*

Following pages:
Fig. 124. DEADMANS BLACK-ON-RED. *Ca.* A.D. *800–1000. Height 11.4 cm. Diameter 19.7 cm. Marjorie and Charles Benton Collection, Evanston, Ill. Solid elements appended to long sets of parallel lines are an unusual treatment here. A running zigzag set of parallel lines with solids at the corner areas was more common.*

Fig. 125. CITADEL POLYCHROME. *Ca.* A.D. *1115–1200. Height 14 cm. Diameter 25.4 cm. Museum of New Mexico Collections, Santa Fe. 43328/11. Designs on this deep bowl have been limited to a rectilinear pattern of broad red lines bordered by narrow black lines on an orange background. Large red areas without borders are usually found on the exterior surfaces of bowls of this type.*

Opposite page:
Fig. 122 a–d. MESA VERDE BLACK-ON-WHITE. *Ca.* A.D. *1200–1300. (a) Height 11.4 cm. Diameter 11.4 cm. (b) Height 10.1 cm. Diameter 10.1 cm. (c) Height 10.1 cm. Diameter 10.1 cm. (d) Height 11.4 cm. Diameter 9.5 cm. Marjorie and Charles Benton Collection, Evanston, Ill. These four mugs indicate the variability of design within the same ceramic type and on the same vessel form. The simplicity of the paneled arrangement in the band layout on mug "b" and its closeness to a McElmo style suggest that it may be the older of the group.*

FIGURE 124

FIGURE 125

97

FIGURE 126

of the lines. Nested chevrons, angular frets, and rectangular scrolls occurred, with an occasional use of interlocking curvilinear scrolls extending from solid triangular elements.[74] This style was also characteristic of that found on Piedra Black-on-white.

Tsegi Orange Ware has much the same history as San Juan Red Ware. Differences in the two wares consisted of the use of crushed sherd temper and more uniform orange paste in Tsegi Orange Ware. The ware was abundant along the Colorado River, downstream from the junction with the San Juan River to just below its confluence with the Little Colorado River. Tsegi Orange Ware was a widely traded ware throughout the period from A.D. 1050 to 1300. Paints on the types include black manganese, white kaolin, and red hematite. These were combined in designs that included hatched panels; series of parallel lines that were usually narrow; horizontal and diagonal hatching or rectangular, circular, stepped, or triangular panels; staggered lines; vertical lines with staggered squares; and solid stepped elements. There are nineteen types of this ware, and of these, Tusayan Black-on-red is illustrated here. From Tsegi and other orange wares, bichromes developed into the earliest polychrome styles, two examples of which are Tusayan Polychrome and Citadel Polychrome.

Winslow Orange Ware, a grouping of eight ceramic types confined in large part to the period A.D. 1300 to 1400, had a rather limited distribution, with major concentration in the southern part of the northeast Arizona region along the Little Colorado River and its tributaries.[75] Many types appear to mark the beginning of distinctive styles at a center. Residual or soil clays were used, and the resultant paste was softer than most other pottery from the region. In terms of color, the core varied from pinkish to tan, orange, buff, gray, or an occasional brick-red. The surface was smoothed or polished and either had no slip or a thin, watery slip; black paint was weak and flat, and white paint, when used, was somewhat fugitive.

Jeddito Yellow Ware was first made in the late Prehistoric period, about A.D. 1250, but types in this ware are still made to the present day. Harold S. Colton has remarked

TUSAYAN BLACK-ON-RED. *Ca.* A.D. *1050–1150. Height 17.7 cm. Diameter 22.5 cm. The Heard Museum, Phoenix, Ariz. NA-SW-AZ-A3-48. Extreme simplicity of design distinguishes this high-necked jar. A band of triangular and diamond-shaped areas filled with parallel lines was painted on a thick, red-slipped background.*

that early examples did not reveal great changes or special advancements in stylistic techniques.[76] The major changes included the use of yellow-firing clays to form an exceptionally hard vessel wall, and the use of manganese rather than iron-based paint. Temper included rare, very fine quartz sand and red fragments. The types were made in the general vicinity of the present Hopi pueblos in northeastern Arizona but were traded widely over the major part of the inhabited sections of the Southwest.

Pottery types of the White Mountain Red Ware, the most abundant and widely distributed ware, were made in greatest frequency in the high country that presently extends along the Arizona–New Mexico boundary between Highway I-40 on the north and the headwaters of the Salt River to the south. They were made in what was once the

Cibola White Ware region. Early black-on-white types developed in the northern part of the region but, through time, there was a shift in the manufacturing centers toward the south-southwest so that the latest types were most abundantly found in the Upper Salt River drainage. The origin of their red slip background is still conjectural, but it has been determined that all of the attributes characteristic of the earliest White Mountain Red Ware, except for the red slip, existed previously in the Cibola White Ware region. Therefore, a rediscovery of the oxidizing atmosphere for firing pottery seems probable.

A detailed study of the ware is found in Roy L. Carlson's work.[77] He has distinguished six partly sequential and developmentally related styles among the fifteen pottery types included in the ware. Significantly, styles cut across the White Mountain Red Ware "types." These types are defined by varying combinations of white and black paints on exterior and interior surfaces, but elements and motifs are somewhat independent of the different paint and surface treatments, and some styles are in fact derived from black-on-white types.

The Holbrook style, made from A.D. 1100 to 1150, was one of the earliest to appear and was mostly used on black-on-red but occasionally on polychrome types. Holbrook — or, more accurately, Black Mesa style — employed solid motifs arranged in a band without double framing lines. Characteristic motifs were joined or interlocked ribbon-like frets with either plain or barbed ends. Dots were sometimes pendant to the frets, but other elaborations were absent. The opposed frets were symmetrically arranged along the bands.

A temporal equivalent of the Holbrook style was the Puerco style, made from A.D. 1000 to 1200. The most common example was Puerco Black-on-red, but the style was also found on polychrome wares. The Puerco style combined either solid and vertical hatched motifs that did not interlock, or solid and checkerboard motifs with no hatched units. Motifs were organized within a single or double band layout, and framing lines were on both the top and bottom of the bands. Vertical hatching, or parallel lines, divided

the band into sections so that solid motifs alternated with hatching. The solids used included checkerboards, negative rectangles, frets with pendant dots, negative diamonds and zigzags, and barbed ends. On polychromes, the white paint was used on the exterior of bowls in running, wide line-designs; massive white motifs, such as a hand, were sometimes used as an outline in a simple, glaze paint line.

FIGURE 127

PUERCO BLACK-ON-RED. *Ca. A.D. 1000–1200. Height 11 cm. Diameter 26 cm. The American Museum of Natural History, N.Y. H/11525. Distinctive of Puerco Black-on-red is a design style with opposed units. This example has broad lines forming a rectilinear scroll that terminates in heavier stepped elements.*

Following pages:

Fig. 128. WINGATE BLACK-ON-RED. *Ca. A.D. 1125–1200. Height 10 cm. Diameter 26.5 cm. The Heard Museum, Phoenix, Ariz. NA-SW-AZ-A3-43. Although the background color of this bowl is similar to that of Puerco Black-on-red, the design is composed of contrasting hatched and solid figures in a band arrangement. The space left in the bottom of this bowl is square but was sometimes circular on other examples.*

Fig. 129. QUERINO POLYCHROME. *Ca. A.D. 1125–1200. Height 9.5 cm. Diameter 21 cm. Arizona State Museum, University of Arizona, Tucson. 19774. What may be an early representation of symbols distinctive to ceramic production centers often appears on bowl exteriors of this type. Here, red circles with an interior cross have been painted on a cream-colored slip background. This type is often considered a variety of Wingate Polychrome.*

FIGURE 128

100

FIGURE 129

FIGURE 130

ST. JOHNS BLACK-ON-RED. *Ca. A.D. 1175–1300. Height 12.7 cm. Diameter 29.5 cm. Fred Harvey Collection, The Heard Museum, Phoenix, Ariz. 342-P. The repetition of opposed solid and hatched interlocked rectangular scrolls on this vessel is identical to patterns found on many Tularosa Black-on-white examples. This bowl differs from St. Johns Polychrome only in the absence of white line decorations on the exterior.*

The Wingate style, made from A.D. 1000 to 1200, introduced the interlocked solid and hatched units that were present on Wingate Black-on-red, early Wingate Polychrome, and sometimes on St. Johns Polychrome. This was essentially the style of Reserve Black-on-white. The solid units were most frequently a barbed scroll, but plain or stepped edges, and dots or negative circles with dots, were also found. The hatched units were a mirror image of the solids but were filled with diagonal lines and were somewhat wider than the solids. In most cases, the layout was a band that was not divided into panels and which sometimes covered the entire bowl interior. The use of white paint on polychromes was confined to the exterior decoration on bowls.

Tularosa style, again paralleling that of contemporaneous black-on-white wares, was made from A.D. 1200 to 1300. It was characterized by a band layout that left the bottom of the bowl open; motifs were repeated from six to eight times around the band, and panel divisions were only rarely present. The solid motifs emphasized wide lines in the form of scrolls, double terraces, frets with stepped ends, and vertical zigzags. Opposed motifs were hatched with thin, closely-spaced diagonal lines, as well as with lines parallel to the framing lines or a combination of both. On the polychromes, white paint was used to outline elements on both the interior and exterior of bowls, or it sometimes formed the entire design on the bowl exterior.

The Pinedale style, made from A.D. 1300 to 1400, was developed out of the Tularosa style. It appeared on Pinedale Polychrome, Pinedale Black-on-red, Cedar Creek Polychrome, and, occasionally, St. Johns Polychrome. The common layout was unsectioned bands in which the patterns were symmetrical with repeated motifs; repetition usually occurred no more than four times, instead of the six to eight times on the Tularosa style. The units were much larger, and the solids were as wide as the hatched ones. Elaboration of the edges of the units gave way to an emphasis on complex filler devices, one of which was the squiggle line. The running diamond and small pendant birds or parrot figures appeared, made by adding a curved beak, legs, and a tail to a triangle. The white paint on polychromes was still used primarily for outlining the motifs on the interior of bowls, but it occasionally formed complex units on the exterior, independent of the black paint.

A radically different concept was used in the Four Mile style, made from A.D. 1300 to 1400 or 1450 and found on Four Mile Polychrome, Showlow Polychrome, Kinishba Polychrome, and Point of Pines Polychrome. The focus of

Opposite page:
Fig. 131. FOUR MILE POLYCHROME. *Ca. A.D. 1300–1400. Height 10.5 cm. Diameter 26.5 cm. The Heard Museum, Phoenix, Ariz. NA-SW-Mg-A7–4. The interior of this bowl was painted with a fine white outline to produce the asymmetrical design. The sweeping scroll was part of the stylized bird motifs in many later types.*

FIGURE 131

attention shifted from the bowl wall to the center of the bowl, with the use of large single motifs. Divisions of the field still existed, and there was occasional repetition of like units or alternation of unlike units. Many pieces lacked bilateral symmetry when the field was divided into unlike areas, and the organization of the design frequently left out opposed similarly-shaped units. Internal elaboration in motifs included parallel hatched elements, stepped line fillers, negative stepped units, dots, and occasional patches of white paint. Geometric figures began to evolve into biomorphic forms, especially birds. White paint as well as black was used to form outlines or filler designs on the bowl interior. On the exterior, white motifs sometimes formed a band framed by wide black lines. On Showlow Polychrome, the interior surface of bowls was slipped white to form the field on which black paint was applied; the exterior remained red slipped and was decorated with a band of black and white motifs.

The White Mountain Red Ware was not the only group of polychromes found on the Colorado Plateau during late prehistoric times. Although they were extremely rare, polychromes were produced in the northern Southwest. Similarly, there are sites in the Anasazi area whose inhabitants seem to have imported abundant polychromes distinctive of Mogollon and even Hohokam areas. These Salado polychromes are still the subject of much dispute.

One of the most intriguing aspects of polychromes is their diverse technology and art style. There were some types that were so homogeneous both stylistically and technologically that they can only be interpreted as the product of one or a few nearby communities whose potters were in close contact with one another and produced vessels for distribution over a widespread area. At the same time, there were types that had extremely standardized styles but highly varied technology. This is perhaps best explained by the possible existence of itinerant potters, although it could have resulted from the widespread exchange of materials used in ceramic manufacture. Both instances suggest a significant increase in specialization in ceramic production.

The complexity of different technological and design patterns is an accurate reflection of organizational variation during this period. A few large sites, some with thousands of rooms, dominated surrounding areas. Alliance networks linked such sites along east-west and north-south axes that crosscut much of the Southwest. Pottery-making was certainly specialized, although to what extent is only now being explored. It is not improbable that the distribution of polychrome wares directly reflects economic and political competition between the inhabitants of sites and districts in the prehistoric Southwest.

In summary, scholars have learned that the original idea for and design of Southwestern ceramics was a Mesoamerican concept. When decorations were first applied on Southwestern pottery, however, the background selected was a locally developed grayware. At least two major style concepts were evident in even the earliest examples; one probably derived from basketry designs already familiar to the potters, and the other duplicated motifs and layout forms found on painted pottery produced by Mogollon peoples. Individual vessels showed an emphasis on one style or the other, or sometimes they combined units from both. A decorative style became widespread as it crossed large geographical areas and extended to different ceramic types. There must have been either widespread interaction of peoples who were still somewhat mobile, or, at the same time, possibly only relatively few but large population groups were actually engaged in ceramic decoration. Therefore, archaeologists define distinctions among the various types of pottery, in large part, by differences in paint and temper characteristics rather than by changes in art style.

Opposite page:
Fig. 132. KINISHBA POLYCHROME. *Ca.* A.D. *1300–1350. Height 10.2 cm. Diameter 23.4 cm. The Heard Museum, Phoenix, Ariz. NA-SW-AZ-A7–39. Many examples of this type have a light background on the interior, but this bowl illustrates a close relation to Pinedale Polychrome. A distinctive feature is the use of a second red paint on the exterior design.*

FIGURE 132

FIGURE 133

Initial trends in design evolution involved the development of contrasts; solid elements became larger and bounding lines became finer. About A.D. 900 to 950, enough change had taken place so that regional differentiation was evident, even though design styles in the general sense continued to cross regions and ceramic types. The amount of variability suggests that ceramics were being produced in more centers as peoples became less migratory. Nevertheless, recent studies of rainfall distribution indicate that populations remaining in a limited area faced uncertain crop yield and probably would not have survived without an extended trade network.[78] This interaction may be responsible for similarities in art forms over a large part of the Colorado Plateau.

Redwares appeared on the Colorado Plateau by A.D. 700. Although there were fewer pieces than the number of black-on-white vessels, the color appears to have been important. Many potters producing early grayware types attempted to copy the redware by the application of a fugitive red slip. Popularity of the red background increased through time so that by the 1000s, a variety of forms were created, even though decorative styles tended to follow those of the black-on-white types. Emil W. Haury has suggested, based on his research in southern Arizona, an association of the color red with water, a concept similar to one in Mesoamerica.[79] If that attitude prevailed in the Pueblo area, the importance of water in relation to increased emphasis on settled communities would have resulted in greater use of red. The last of the 1000s and most of the 1100s were moisture-deficient, and this was a time of great redware expansion.

The end of the 1000s and the 1100s was also the time when large population centers were built in many parts of the Pueblo area. Growth of centers and the beginning of complex societies were accompanied by an increasing diversity of styles among the regions. At the same time, relatively characteristic styles appeared at the larger centers. It seems that artistic creativity in the pueblos was at the highest level when social interaction both within and between communities existed at an intense level.[80] At Chaco Canyon, Chaco Black-on-white was distinctive and represented a pattern departure from previous styles. Similarly, Mesa Verde Black-on-white evolved into a unique style. At this point, the spread of vessels may have been the result of a formalized trade network. Redwares and polychromes began to replace black-on-white decorated pottery in central-eastern Arizona and central-western New Mexico; in northeastern Arizona, redwares and orangewares dominated painted ceramics by the end of the Prehistoric period.

In the last 125 years of the Prehistoric period, ending about 1400, there were large scale population dislocations that affected all parts of the Southwest. Migration, realignment of social relations, and stress contributed to dramatic reevaluations in the arts. Both the Mesa Verde region and the Upper San Juan River region were without occupants by A.D. 1300, and the progressive abandonment of the Chaco Basin was complete by about the same time. Large-scale population relocations were evident in northeastern Arizona, central-eastern Arizona, and central-western New Mexico. By 1400, there were concentrations of peoples in a few districts such as the Hopi region, Zuñi, and Ácoma. In the Rio Grande region, the early 1300s were characterized by a population increase far in excess of normal reproduction. The beginning of the Protohistoric period, then, was one of readjustment.

Opposite page:
Fig. 133. SHOWLOW POLYCHROME. Ca. A.D. 1300–1400. Height 12 cm. Diameter 14 cm. The Heard Museum, Phoenix, Ariz. NA-SW-Mg-A7–13. This type is distinguished by the use of contrasting red and white background slips. Although the motifs appear on other White Mountain Red Ware types, the arrangement of the pattern in relation to the white slip area on this example is unique.

Pueblo Pottery:
The Protohistoric and Historic Periods

AS HAS BEEN PREVIOUSLY NOTED, the Prehistoric and Historic periods were characterized by change. Almost all parts of the Pueblo world experienced a period of population growth and aggregation during the 1200s. Many centers came into existence as peoples in various districts banded together to form large social units, and under such conditions there was an accompanying increase in the scale of interaction between villages as well as within the villages themselves. One effect was the development of numerous ceramics that came to symbolize particular communities. The 1300s were a period of stress: many demographic relocations took place; some regions were abandoned, while others experienced rapid population growth. Overall, there may have been a decline in the total number of people.

There is little agreement among investigators as to specific causes for these changes. Drought, arroyo cutting that destroyed arable lands, changes in the rainfall that shortened the growing season in the higher elevations, failure of the Mesoamerican trade network, and even enemy peoples have been considered as possible reasons. It is probable that no single cause explains all cases. But there is agree-ment that stresses of many kinds played major roles in the responses to change made by Pueblo Indians.

The events of the Protohistoric and Historic periods did not occur at the same time in all districts, nor were all districts affected equally. Each had a unique history. The events varied from the aggregation of related peoples who came together from a widespread region into a few large pueblos, to the progressive movement of people from remote regions into occupied areas. External factors were added when Europeans began to settle in the Southwest and when Athapascans or other Indian groups made inroads into the Pueblo area. In the case of the Spanish occupation, there was an attempt at directed culture change.

The Protohistoric period was the time when many of the present Pueblo groups became identified with a particular district. After the abandonment of major parts of the Southwest such as Mesa Verde and the Chaco Basin, and subsequent resettlement, many of the new homelands have remained the ones with which groups are associated today.

The Hopi people appear to have been associated with northeastern Arizona for as long as the Anasazi tradition can be identified. Hopi ceramics of the Prehistoric period were virtually unique in that ceramic developments of the Protohistoric and Historic periods continued the regional trends noted earlier and displayed very few significant changes. Specializations within the group are evident, and there are distinctive variations in the basic theme. More than any other ceramic, Jeddito Black-on-yellow becomes the model from which the variations emerge.

Variations are quite numerous, depending on the level of investigation of stylistic diversity. Stippled and engraved varieties are recognized, as well as polychromes using white or red paint along with black. Red paint polychrome — Sikyatki Polychrome, made between 1400 and 1625 — is thought by some to have been associated with the arrival of the kachina cult in the area.

The popularity of Jeddito Black-on-yellow and its derivatives is expressed in the fact that pieces characteristic of the type are found over most of the Southwest occupied at that time. The type was most abundant in the interval from 1325 to 1600, although derivatives have continued to be made up to the present.

The transition from the Prehistoric to the Protohistoric period in the Zuñi region was marked by a great many changes in the archaeological record. Some alterations — such as the concentration of people into fewer but larger pueblos, often located on the summit of a mesa — appear to have been a continuation of events that began earlier. The disappearance of round kivas and their ultimate replacement by square kivas in house blocks, the start of cremation of the dead, and the probable introduction of the unique Zuñian language about this time all have been advanced as new cultural attributes, with no previous basis in the region. Similarly, ceramics underwent significant changes in style.

Wherever the new peoples and cultural items came from, the Zuñi were living in seven to ten large towns at the time of contact. The Zuñi towns are generally thought to be the cities of Cibola that the Spanish mistakenly believed were plastered with gold. Total agreement regarding the events involved in the changes does not exist. Neverthe-

less, any explanation of these events must take into account the relationship of the Prehistoric period remains in the Zuñi region to those in the larger Cibola White Ware region, of which the Zuñi region was a part. It remains to be clarified to what extent the earlier population had been replaced, had joined with an incoming group, or had merely changed because of the adoption of ideas from peoples who had moved from nearby localities during the last of the Prehistoric period. These new orientations were

FIGURE 134

JEDDITO BLACK-ON-YELLOW. *Ca.* A.D. *1325–1600. Height 9 cm. Diameter 18 cm. Arizona State Museum, University of Arizona, Tucson. GP-11681. Although they were not common, unusually shaped vessels such as this form with two openings were occasionally made. The decorative style is early geometric; naturalistic motifs became dominant in later vessels of this type.*

Following pages:
Fig. 135. SIKYATKI POLYCHROME. *Ca.* A.D. *1400–1625. Height 25.4 cm. Diameter 36.8 cm. Marjorie and Charles Benton Collection, Evanston, Ill. The primary difference between this type and Jeddito Black-on-yellow is the addition of red paint to the design. Otherwise, the geometric decorative style on this jar is equivalent. A good example of a line break is illustrated.*

Fig. 136. SIKYATKI POLYCHROME. *Ca.* A.D. *1400–1625. Height 16.5 cm. Diameter 33 cm. Field Museum of Natural History, Chicago, Ill. 21174. This canteen displays the representation of a kachina. A prominent mask occupies the upper half of the vessel, while the lower part of the figure is represented by stylized feathers.*

FIGURE 135

FIGURE 136

III

FIGURE 137

Top:

Fig. 137. SAN BERNARDO POLY-CHROME. *Ca. 1628–1680. Height 20 cm. Diameter 30.5 cm. Peabody Museum, Harvard University, Cambridge, Mass. Thomas V. Keam Collection. 43-39-10/25131. San Bernardo Polychrome is an extremely variable composite of a number of traditions. The vessel form is suggestive of later Keresan-influenced Payupki Polychrome. The designs are a combination of Hopi Sikyatki Polychrome and Eastern Pueblo motifs.*

Bottom:

Fig. 138. HESHOTAUTHLA BLACK-ON-RED. *Ca. A.D. 1275–1400. Height. 9 cm. Diameter 19.5 cm. The American Museum of Natural History, N.Y. 29.0/6487. An unusual feature of this design is the alternate filling of square and triangular panels. When this layout was used, the triangular spaces often were not decorated. The use of parallel lines with pendant dots is a frequent motif on this type.*

Opposite page:

Fig. 139. GILA POLYCHROME. *Ca. A.D. 1250–1400. Height 15.7 cm. Diameter 28 cm. Marjorie and Charles Benton Collection, Evanston, Ill. The role of this type in the development of later Pueblo ceramics is still conjectural. It was frequently found in the Zuñi region, and contrasting slip colors are much like Protohistoric period Zuñi vessels. Many of the motifs seen on this bowl are even used on contemporary western Pueblo ceramics.*

FIGURE 138

FIGURE 139

FIGURE 140

FIGURE 141

Opposite page:

Fig. 140. KWAKINA POLYCHROME. *Ca.* A.D. *1325–1400. Height 10.5 cm. Diameter 24.7 cm. Museum of the American Indian, Heye Foundation, N.Y. Hendricks-Hodge Expedition, 13/2008. This type is characterized by contrasting surface colors of white on the interior and red on the exterior. The opposed, stepped, glaze-paint elements were derived from a long-standing tradition, while the exterior white zig-zag line is found on the earlier St. Johns Polychrome.*

Right:

Fig. 141. PINNAWA GLAZE-ON-WHITE. *Ca.* A.D. *1350–1450. Height 17.8 cm. Diameter 25 cm. Museum of the American Indian, Heye Foundation, N.Y. 13/ 981. The simple geometric glaze-paint decorations on this jar appear to have developed from Kwakina Polychrome. Red was not used either as a slip or as part of the design. (See appendix, p. 143)*

reflected in the ceramics, which continued to change in style development throughout the Protohistoric and Historic periods.

Given the relatively dramatic changes that occurred, it is interesting to note the presence of Salado pottery in some protohistoric Zuñi sites. The polychromes of the Salado tradition — Pinto, Gila, and Tonto — were characterized by a white slip on the interior of bowls and a red slip on the exterior. Carbon pigments predominated. Distinctions among the three are based on characteristics of the slip, and varied use of red in the design. The Salado polychromes were among the most widely distributed painted types in the prehistoric Southwest. They have been found as far north as the Zuñi area, as far south as northern Mexico, are present in Classic period Hohokam sites on the west, and are occasionally seen as far east as the Rio Grande Valley. Sites in which they have been found in any great quantity are rare, but it is of interest that some of the highest concentrations are in late prehistoric and early historic sites

near Zuñi — for example, at Table Rock Pueblo.[81] Since these types were almost certainly not of local manufacture, they may indicate the movement of new peoples into the area just before the founding of the large Zuñi towns.

Following pages:

Fig. 142. HAWIKUH POLYCHROME. *Ca. 1630–1680. Height 13 cm. Diameter 23.5 cm. Museum of the American Indian, Heye Foundation, N.Y. Hendricks-Hodge Expedition, 7/5574. The pronounced bulge in the upper wall of this vessel and the strong slope of the lower body contour are form concepts that probably originated in the Rio Grande region. The stylized bird motif is distinctly western in concept, however.*

Fig. 143. KECHIPAWAN POLYCHROME. *Ca.* A.D. *1375–1425. Height 7.7 cm. Diameter 18 cm. Museum of the American Indian, Heye Foundation, N.Y. Hendricks-Hodge Expedition, 8/6397. Both surfaces of this bowl were covered with a white slip, and red paint was only used in the spaces in the design, which includes stylized feathers and birds.*

FIGURE 142

FIGURE 143

KIAPKWA POLYCHROME. *Ca. 1750–1850. Height 26 cm. Diameter 33.5 cm. The American Museum of Natural History, N.Y. 50/413. This vessel displays the use of many earlier but modified design motifs. The terraced units, volutes, and pointed feathers continued into Zuñi Polychrome.*

FIGURE 144

St. Johns Polychrome, a White Mountain Red Ware type discussed earlier, was also very widespread. It was from St. Johns Polychrome that the earliest protohistoric Zuñi designs seem to have been derived. (The same is true of similar developments that occurred earlier in the Rio Grande area.) The earliest such form was Heshotauthla Polychrome, a local glaze rendering of St. Johns Polychrome that was made from A.D. 1275 to about 1400. Subsequent types in the Zuñi area usually had glazes. While some types imitated White Mountain Red Ware rather directly, others reflected an admixture of both Salado and White Mountain Red Ware types.

After 1680, with the events of the Pueblo Rebellion and the following reconquest by the Spanish, glaze paint disappeared and the later Zuñi ceramics had matte paints.

There was a short-term revival of glaze decorated pottery, Hawikuh Polychrome, from about 1630 to 1680 or slightly later. It is believed that the type is a reintroduction from the Rio Grande, since there is no evidence of continuity of glazes in the Zuñi region between Kechipawan Polychrome and this type.

It is difficult to say whether these influences represent the influx of peoples from distant sites, copying from distant traditions, or actually copying designs taken from prehistoric sites. But some sensitivity to the design traditions of the ancients clearly existed. Kiapkwa Polychrome, made between about 1700 and 1850, reflected a return to the opposed solid and hatched motifs that had been the standard of the Cibola White Ware artists.

The advent of longer winter seasons after 1325 brought

about population movement to lower elevations within the Pueblo region. As a result, many settlements in the higher sections were abandoned, and an influx of people was evident at Ácoma Pueblo as well as nearby centers and sites along the Rio San José. Arable lands were not available to even the most advantageously situated pueblos, however, so there was increased use of seasonally occupied farming sites, which were as many as ten miles or more away from the home pueblo. Such a system was effective in permitting centralized locations to grow, since they were not dependent upon adjacent resources. When the Spanish first entered the Pueblo region, the majority of people were concentrated at Ácoma. Nevertheless, documents from the early part of the Historic period describe the cultivation of crops along the Rio San José by the Ácoma Indians.

Regrouping, centralization, and the accompanying diversification of social roles that can take place in a large unit may be linked to increased communication after 1350. Formal trails were established, and interaction appears to have become more frequent between Ácoma residents and those in the Zuñi region, as well as with Zia Pueblo. The effect of such interaction on local ceramics was evident especially as a result of trade with Zuñi; Zia contacts may have been responsible for the quantities of Rio Grande glazes coming to Ácoma.

Not all the Protohistoric and Historic period events that played a part in Ácoma ceramics were concerned with trade. Near the end of the previous time interval, some peoples from the Mogollon region moved northward and settled with communities in the Ácoma region. The brownwares they brought were reproduced as local copies in both brown and gray clays, but little lasting influence was manifested in the local decorated types. Similarly, some groups moving out of the Chaco Basin brought a carbon-paint decorated pottery, but the style did not replace the use of the local mineral paint.

The interaction network that extended from the Hopi pueblos through the Ácoma region all the way to the Rio Grande is somewhat more important. Unlike the condition at Zuñi, where there was an interval when ceramics were decorated with a matte paint in a Hopi design style, matte paint did not replace glazes at Ácoma. Nevertheless, at Ácoma there were examples of Jeddito Black-on-yellow, Sikyatki Polychrome, and Matsaki Polychrome, although these were never abundant. And yet, design elements from these Hopi ceramics were recognizable on Ácoma pottery and continue in use even today. Somewhat more difficult to evaluate are the effects of the short interval when members of the Zia pueblos lived and farmed along the Rio San José, only to move back home when the dry spell was over. Since interaction between the two peoples has a long history, the situation probably had little additional impact.

The late Prehistoric period ceramics in the Ácoma region have been described earlier as paralleling those from the Zuñi region and of the White Mountain Red Ware region. A continuation of the similarities is evident in the Protohistoric period, when Ácoma decorated ceramics can be confused with those produced at Zuñi. While distinctions can be made for purposes of determining origin, the overall similarities are striking.

In 1599, Vicente de Zaldivar conquered Ácoma. Approximately five hundred men, women, and children were taken back with him to Santo Domingo Pueblo, where a trial was held because of Ácoma involvement in the earlier

Following pages:
Fig. 145. HAWIKUH GLAZE-ON-RED. *Ca. 1630–1680. Height 25.4 cm. Diameter 34.3 cm. School of American Research, Santa Fe, N.M. Indian Arts Fund. IAF 1031. The design styles and vessel shapes are essentially the same for this type and Hawikuh Polychrome, but the Glaze-on-red background color, which covers the entire surface of the vessel, is different. This example is actually a twentieth-century replica, but exact in every detail. It was probably made at Ácoma.*

Fig. 146. McCARTYS POLYCHROME. *Ca. 1850–1875. Height 28 cm. Diameter 28 cm. Marjorie and Charles Benton Collection, Evanston, Ill. Bold and often garish decorations are found on this type. This is a late example, but it illustrates the incorporation of non-Ácoma elements. The large circles are probably of Laguna origin, and the diagonal parallel lines with interior dots are from Tewa Polychrome in the Rio Grande region.*

FIGURE 145

FIGURE 146

FIGURE 147

LAGUNA POLYCHROME. *Ca. 1830–1900. Height 23.5 cm. Diameter 29.8 cm. Museum of New Mexico Collections, Santa Fe. 18704/12. Designs of this type display an unmistakable ancestry in the symmetric tradition at Ácoma. Motifs were heavier, however, and combined in a band of interconnected forms with a lavish use of red.*

FIGURE 148

McCARTYS POLYCHROME. *Ca. 1850–1890. Height 24.1 cm. Diameter 30.5 cm. Museum of New Mexico Collections, Santa Fe. 12042/12. On this vessel, naturalistic floral motifs bounded by large sweeping curves, similar to Zia Polychrome, replaced the earlier solid curvilinear figures.*

death of Vicente's brother. The prisoners were sentenced to various lengths of servitude, and a number of girls were sent to convents in Mexico City. In the first half of the 1600s, when the people started returning to Ácoma, their association with the northern Rio Grande peoples was reflected in the ceramics that began to be produced, especially in vessel shapes. The pronounced bulge around the mid-section of jars was characteristic; indented bases, however, did not become popular until near the end of the 1600s. Some of these innovations in form were also passed on to the Zuñi.

Decorative aspects, on the other hand, did not show evidence of the Rio Grande styles. Stylized feathers, terraced figures, and birds were found on most vessels, and the bird renditions bore many resemblances to those from the Hopi region. The exclusive use of a red slip was a variation on the use of both white and red slips on zones of the vessels.[82] Although the types are referred to as Hawikuh Polychrome or Hawikuh Glaze-on-red because the first descriptions are from examples recovered in the Zuñi region, the impetus for the development may have reached the Zuñi region from Ácoma.

Laguna Pueblo became an entity in the Reconquest period following the Pueblo Rebellion of 1680. Some people from Ácoma were included in the makeup of the settlement, and the ceramics made before 1830 are difficult to distinguish on a design basis from those at Ácoma. A recognizable Laguna Polychrome, which retained many features of Acomita Polychrome, was made after that time. The heavy motifs were combined into a band of interconnected forms with a lavish use of red. The walls were thick;

FIGURE 149

MATSAKI POLYCHROME. *Ca.* A.D. *1475–1680. Height 16 cm. Diameter 18.5 cm. Museum of the American Indian, Heye Foundation, N.Y. Hendricks-Hodge Expedition, 8/6258. Although this type is thought to have been inspired by Hopi ceramic designs, the heavier elements lend it a distinctive character. Decorations on this small jar lack the precise draftsmanship of contemporary Hopi vessels.*

the paste contained crushed sherd but also sand; and dark fragments and polishing often left visible marks on the slip. Although Laguna Polychrome was an important type in the late 1800s, it declined significantly and is almost negligible in the Modern period.[83]

Interesting, then, in retrospect, is the case of Matsaki Polychrome in the Zuñi area. Zuñi legends indicate the movement of some Zuñi to Hopi lands during this period. Abandonment of glaze paint and the adoption of a distinctively different style were both evident in Matsaki Polychrome from 1475 to late in the 1600s. The smooth hard surface of previous ceramics gave way to a somewhat rough or crazed surface over a crumbly paste. A background color of buff to orange, cream, or yellow-brown was decorated in complex geometric and feather designs using a dark brown or black and a reddish-brown paint. The styles re-

semble those of Sikyatki Polychrome of the Hopi region, but the brushwork was of poorer quality. Bowl interiors were the primary field utilized, and only simple elements appeared on bowl exteriors. On jars, the decorative field extended from the shoulder almost to the rim. What may be considered a variety of Matsaki Polychrome was distinguished by the absence of red paint. It is possible that this was a purposeful deviation, since the vessel forms represented in the many pieces recovered, copied European models in cups, jars, and bowls. The atypical shapes may also indicate that Matsaki Brown-on-buff was relatively more common after European contacts.[84] Matsaki Polychrome, then, reflected contact that took place with several culturally different groups.

The late thirteenth century and the early fourteenth century in the Rio Grande region was an interval marked by the entry of peoples from far-flung sections of the Pueblo area. At first, newcomers settled in the outlying margins of the Rio Grande Valley. Numbers of large communities, many of which may have had a population of over one thousand people, came into existence along the Rio Chama, on the Pajarito Plateau, the Rio Jemez, in the Galisteo Basin, and on the east side of the Manzano Mountains. Especially those groups along the Rio Chama and on the Pajarito Plateau slowly gravitated toward the Rio Grande Valley proper. Meanwhile, the small sites of the earlier inhabitants were either abandoned or experienced growth as peoples moved together into the larger pueblos. The process effectively reduced the land area over which the indigenous groups were distributed. It is possible that a condition approaching equilibrium had been reached by the time of the first Spanish explorations of the Rio Grande Valley in 1540.

After the disappointments of the Coronado expedition, there was little interest in the northern lands, and colonization was not attempted until 1598. It was then that Don Juan de Oñate brought settlers to a site adjacent to the Pueblo known today as San Juan. By 1610, however, the colony had moved to Santa Fe. Although the numbers of Europeans remained small during the early seventeenth century, the Franciscan Order did pursue an active campaign of mission construction and conversion of the Indians. The missions, which were located adjacent to or in a large pueblo, or as a center around which a pueblo was built, became the outposts of Spanish activity and control. By 1680, factors brought about by the Spanish domination resulted in the Pueblo Rebellion and the retreat of the Spanish from the province. It was not until 1692 that Diego de Vargas mounted a successful reconquest.

Both the Pueblo Rebellion and the reconquest gave rise to major dislocations among the Pueblo Indians. Groups moved from the Galisteo Basin to the Hopi region, where the pueblo of Hano was established by speakers of Tewa. Similarly, members of Sandia Pueblo lived in the Hopi region for a time. People in the Jemez locality, along with some of their allies, fled northward to the Gobernador district, where they remained for about fifty years; the present Jemez Pueblo was established when they returned. Other groups from the Rio Grande sought refuge westward at the site that became Laguna. Ultimately, the conditions became relatively stabilized, and while insurrections did occur, none compares with the magnitude of the Pueblo Rebellion.

Each of the events summarized above is correlated with significant directional changes in ceramic decoration. Even the more subtle shifts in policy during the Mexican period and the later period of American control seemed to find expression in ceramic art. Some verged on nativistic movements, while others began to reflect the economic changes of the late nineteenth century. Nevertheless, cultural heritage in expression was a theme that is recognizable throughout.

Initially, as new groups came to the Rio Grande, they brought pottery from their prior homeland or attempted to duplicate it with local resources. This condition was short-lived; in the early to middle of the fourteenth century, many new decorative motif combinations reflecting a syncretism of local and intrusive elements came into existence. Also, the distinction between northern and southern sections of the Rio Grande Valley became more marked, with the division zone near La Bajada Hill, between Albu-

querque and Santa Fe. To the north, most of the subsequent pottery types were black-on-white with the use of black carbon paint; in the south, glaze and, later, mineral paints were dominant.

The glaze decorated types developed out of the White Mountain Red Ware. Especially St. Johns Polychrome, St. Johns Glaze-polychrome, and Heshotauthla Polychrome appear to have been within the tradition from which the first glaze-on-red types evolved. Distinctions that separated Los Padillas Glaze-polychrome were minimal enough so that many researchers see the former as at most a variety of the latter. But by 1350, Agua Fria Glaze-on-red appeared, the first of the types in the Rio Grande Glaze A group. Its designs departed significantly from the St. Johns style. On the interior of bowls and below the neck on jars there was a paneled band with wide or narrow oblique lines, solid triangles and stepped keys, solid rectilinear units, or checkerboard areas. Hatched figures were missing. A simple figure was sometimes painted at the bottom of the bowl interior, and glaze-paint paired slashes or a cross were sometimes found on a bowl exterior.[85]

The temper used in all of the Rio Grande Glaze A types was predominantly crushed igneous rock, but individual pieces differed in the type of rock depending on the source. Petrographic analyses indicate that only a limited number of possible sources were used. Researchers therefore infer that specialized production and distribution centers for pottery had again come into existence. If this is true, the reorganization of such centers must have taken place rapidly after the disruptions at the end of the Prehistoric period. In addition to the change in location of manufacturing centers, population movements were the reason for

Opposite page:
Fig. 150. RIO GRANDE GLAZE C, ESPINOSA GLAZE-POLY-CHROME. *Ca.* A.D. *1450–1500. Height 13 cm. Diameter 29.8 cm. The Heard Museum, Phoenix, Ariz. NA-SW-AZ-A7-16. This bowl has a very light background with rich red paint outlined with glaze paint. Stylized bird motifs are pendant to the rim band on the interior and shown as independent motifs on the exterior.*

FIGURE 150

FIGURE 151   FIGURE 152

the use of yellowish to whitish slips on some types. Nevertheless, opinions differ as to the point of origin. Some researchers argue for a source in the Jeddito Yellow Ware tradition; others contend that it came from the Casas Grandes region in Mexico when people moved away from that ceramic center.

Rio Grande Glaze B began at about 1425 and was characterized by a rim form on bowls that exhibited a distinct thickening at the top. Siltstone and sand were used as temper in addition to the crushed igneous rock. Designs were still organized within a paneled band, but the elements tended to be somewhat heavier than in the previous types. The paint continued to be thin, black, and lustrous, and it only rarely ran. In contrast with the diversity of the Glaze A group, there were only four Glaze B types, all closely related. It is possible that this apparent decrease indicates a reduction in a number of pueblos making decorated ceramics and that the distribution system became better established. Another indication that styles may have become characteristic of particular population units was the continuation of Pottery Mound Glaze-polychrome of the Glaze A group through both the Rio Grande Glaze B and C periods.

Espinosa Glaze-polychrome, Rio Grande Glaze C, appeared about 1450 and seemed to have been the product of

Left:

Fig. 151. RIO GRANDE GLAZE A, AGUA FRIA GLAZE-ON-RED. *Ca.* A.D. *1350–1425. Height 11.4 cm. Diameter 26.6 cm. Museum of New Mexico Collections, Santa Fe. 42935/11. Simple geometric elements arranged within panels of a band and drawn with black glaze paint on a red background are characteristic of this type. Although the type developed from western glazes, the design style on this bowl is distinctly similar to concepts in the Rio Grande region.*

Right:

Fig. 152. RIO GRANDE GLAZE B, LARGO GLAZE-POLYCHROME. *Ca.* A.D. *1425–1475. Height 12.5 cm. Diameter 28.5 cm. The American Museum of Natural History, N.Y. 29.0/4351. Organized in a band, the design on this bowl consists of repeated panels drawn with dark brown glaze on a yellow background on the interior, while glaze-outlined elements filled with red occur on the exterior surface.*

Opposite page:

Fig. 153. RIO GRANDE GLAZE D, SAN LAZARO GLAZE-POLYCHROME. *Ca.* A.D. *1490–1550. Height 9.4 cm. Diameter 22.5 cm. Byron Harvey Collection, The Heard Museum, Phoenix, Ariz. 1974.1.23. A lack of contrast between the red paint and the dark slip characterizes this type as a subdued polychrome. By thickening and raising the rim, new fields for decoration were created. In this example, the rim is filled by an elongated zigzag glaze line. The dominant motif on the vessel is a central red-filled cross outlined with glaze paint.*

FIGURE 153

127

one pueblo or a small number of pueblos. Almost the only temper that has been identified by petrographic studies was a hornblende tuff, which was limited in its geological occurrence.[86] This suggests highly localized and specialized production. Characteristic of the bowls were everted to recurved rims with prominent thickening on the rim interior. The glaze paint that was used rarely ran, but it did vary in color from brownish-black to greenish or yellow; the red paint had a rich color. Painted decorations were executed on a white-slipped background, but the surface below the area with designs on both jars and bowls was sometimes slipped red. Espinosa Glaze-polychrome marked the rise of many new motifs, including lines, dots, ticks, checkerboards, crosses, key figures, birds, sunbursts, and terraces. Individual elements were formed by glaze paint or outlined with glaze and filled in with red. In most instances a band, either paneled or not paneled, was the basis for design organization.[87]

Rio Grande Glaze D began about 1490 and has been referred to as a subdued polychrome. A return to the lighter background color similar to that on Rio Grande Glaze C was found on the Rio Grande Glaze E types, which dated from 1515 to the middle of the 1600s.

Rio Grande Glaze E ceramics were being made when the Spanish came into the Rio Grande Valley. There were no changes that can be directly associated with the Coronado expedition, but after Spanish settlements were established in the early seventeenth century, foreign shapes began to appear. Cups and soup plates were added to the shouldered bowls, as were high-necked jars with a bulging mid-section and other unique forms. A concave base on jars may or may not have been a Spanish introduction.[88]

The last of the Rio Grande Glazes, Glaze F, lasted throughout the period from 1650 to 1750, and the many changes evident during this time mark the transition from the Protohistoric period to the Historic period. All utilized a brownish-black or a brown to thick black, runny glaze paint. Rims on the bowls became elongated and formed the zone that was decorated. Simple designs on both the interior and exterior included zigzags, festoons, triangles, and

FIGURE 154

JEMEZ BLACK-ON-WHITE. *Ca.* A.D. *1300–1700. Height 12.7 cm. Diameter 30.5 cm. Museum of New Mexico Collections, Santa Fe. 790/11. This bowl is relatively shallow and has an incurved upper wall and carbon paint decorations on both surfaces. Each panel of the bands is repeated after diagonal line divisions, which are bordered with parallel dashes. Pendant solid triangles border the diagonal lines on the interior panels, and small festoons are pendant to the diagonal line on the exterior.*

oblique lines with pendant birds. The elements were arranged in a band that may or may not have had framing lines, and paneling was rare.

Not all Pueblos participated in the glaze ware tradition, suggesting that some ethnic distinctions were present in the Rio Grande area well before the Pueblo Rebellion. Although the Jemez people lived only a few miles from Zia, the pre-1700 settlements made a distinctive black-on-white pottery decorated with carbon paint on a polished white-slipped surface. It is thought that the style evolved from the earlier Gallina Black-on-white, with a poorly-defined transition type known as Vallecitos Black-on-white. Almost all the Jemez Black-on-white designs appeared in bands on both the interior and exterior of bowls and on the upper wall of jars. There was some degree of paneling, but repetition of motifs was the most common feature. Stylized birds, hourglass figures, birds pendant to oblique

FIGURE 155

FIGURE 156

WIYO BLACK-ON-WHITE. *Ca. A.D. 1325–1400. Height 12.7 cm. Diameter 33.7 cm. Museum of New Mexico Collections, Santa Fe. 35750/11. Large open bowls like this example are frequent forms of this type. Decorations are drawn with carbon paint on an olive drab background and are arranged in a band divided by what has been termed X-sectioning. Repeated alternation of solid and line-filled geometric elements creates contrast.*

BANDELIER BLACK-ON-GRAY. *Ca. A.D. 1400–1500 or 1550. Height 15.2 cm. Diameter 31.4 cm. Museum of New Mexico Collections, Santa Fe. 21903/11. Bowls of this type are decorated on the exterior as well as the interior. The Awanyu is a common design motif. One distinctive feature of the type was the appearance of a large number of jars.*

lines, parallel zigzag lines, crossed lines within rectilinear units, terraced figures, and hooked keys were frequent representations. There was a marked openness to the design structure. When the bottom of the bowl interior was decorated, there was a marked similarity to concepts from the White Mountain Red Ware vessels, both in symmetrical and asymmetrical forms. The bowl and jar forms were frequently alternated with examples of bird effigies.

Jemez Black-on-white exhibited little change from its inception about A.D. 1300 to the time that it ceased to be made during the Pueblo Rebellion interval. After that time, only culinary wares appear to have been made. For their decorated ceramics, the Jemez people seem to have relied upon imported pieces.[89]

Contemporaneous with the glaze paint sequence was a carbon paint tradition of decoration used primarily north of La Bajada Hill. The appearance of the first type, Santa Fe Black-on-white, was described earlier. Many students regard the type as basic to most subsequent developments because of the diversity it had during the span of its existence. There were other distinct types found in the early fourteenth century, however, that may have had a different origin. One is Galisteo Black-on-white, which is possibly closely related to the earlier Mesa Verde Black-on-white by its thick white, well-polished slip, which had a tendency to crackle. Banding was the most prevalent layout for designs, and motifs within the bands included crosshatched geometric figures, hatched stepped elements, large solid lines or rectilinear units, solid saw-tooth figures, lines with pendant dots, and opposed solid and hatched rectilinear motifs. As the type developed, it moved farther and farther away from the Mesa Verde style so that late examples were clearly distinct.[90] Some archaeologists believe that this pattern reflected the migration of Mesa Verde peoples to the Rio Grande.

Wiyo Black-on-white was a local outgrowth of Santa Fe Black-on-white. Abiquiu Black-on-gray, Bandelier Black-on-gray, Cuyamungue Black-on-tan, and Sankawi

Black-on-cream are referred to as Biscuit Ware. The term comes from the thick soft paste, which became widespread in use about 1400. In the initial type, Abiquiu Black-on-gray, almost all pieces were bowls that were polished on the interior but rough on the exterior; only the interior was decorated. Designs were organized into three or four divisions in a band that left the bottom of the bowl plain. Elements included heavy dashes, short bent lines, zigzags, small hatched triangles, checkerboards, crosses, and Awanyus. The latter motif is considered to be related to the plumed serpent of Mesoamerica.

North of the Tewa pueblos are the Tiwa pueblos of Taos and Picuris. Sites in the district that pre-date A.D. 1250 were characterized by mineral paint ceramics, described earlier. When the organic carbon paint type, Santa Fe Black-on-white, appeared in the Rio Grande region, similar black-on-white styles made with local materials followed in the northern districts. Most of the ceramics, however, appear to have been imported from centers to the south. What decorated pottery was made locally was replaced at the time of the Pueblo Rebellion by a micaceous ware made from a brownish- to bronze-colored clay that copied the Jicarilla Apache ceramics. Decoration was confined to applique and/or punched elements. This style continues to be made today and is easily recognized by the glittering surface mica on the brown- to bronze-colored clay.[91]

The dramatic decrease and ultimate abandonment of glaze paint decoration can be linked to the havoc brought about by the Pueblo Rebellion of 1680. Although Rio Grande Glaze F continued to be made into the middle of the 1700s, other ceramics made about 1700 reflected the diversity of interactions among groups during the interval of unrest. Almost the entire population of some districts, such as the Galisteo Basin, relocated in parts of the northern Rio Grande region or in the Hopi region, where the pueblo of Hano was established. One group, Isleta Pueblo, followed the Spanish in their retreat to El Paso. Upon their return to Isleta, the potters brought back a polished redware and a red-on-buff, which lasted until the Modern period. Other peoples fled into areas of refuge for a time

FIGURE 157

GOBERNADOR POLYCHROME. *Ca. 1700–1750. Height 12.1 cm. Diameter 22.2 cm. School of American Research, Santa Fe, N. Mex. Indian Arts Fund. IAF 2162. This type came into existence when diverse groups of peoples were brought together. The simple style exhibits concepts thought to be a combination from many sources, especially from Hopi- and Tewa-style ceramics.*

during the Spanish reconquest and were exposed to a variety of traditions.

The Pueblo revolt and subsequent reconquest provide an interesting case study of the effect of demographic and political stress on art traditions. In 1696, the Jemez people and some of their allies who had resisted the Spanish fled northward to the Gobernador region. For some fifty years, diverse Pueblo peoples and Navajo lived in close proximity. The interactions that took place were oriented toward the west with the Hopi, instead of with the Spanish-occupied regions.

A product of these events was the appearance of a pottery type known as Gobernador Polychrome, in which a number of distinct traditions were combined. It was made until 1750 and is one of the hardest of the Pueblo ceramics. It was decorated in combinations of red, yellow, and black. Most commonly, the elements were black on either a red or yellow background, or the black sometimes outlined red-filled elements. The layout was almost always in paneled bands, with motifs consisting of two or three parallel red bars outlined with black. Narrow black lines were also frequently arranged in vertical, diagonal, horizontal, or crossed units. Triangles appeared where lines met at angles, and sometimes the triangles were fringed. Gobernador Polychrome did not seem to have been important to later Rio Grande designs, but both the early Navajo painted pottery and Payupki Polychrome of the Hopi region strongly resembled it.

Among the Hopi, Payupki Polychrome — made from 1700 to 1800 — reflected their new relationships with the Rio Grande pueblos. People from such pueblos as Sandia and from the Galisteo Basin made their home temporarily or permanently in the Hopi region. In addition, trade relations developed between the Hopi people and groups fleeing from the Spanish reconquest. Payupki Polychrome designs were executed in a pale red and black. Small geometric solids or the outlining of geometric figures were created with black and red, which was used to fill the resulting spaces. The variation in Payupki Polychrome suggests the coming together of a number of traditions.[92]

After the Spanish reconquest of the Rio Grande pueblos in 1694, there is evidence that ceramic traditions became much more a specific village phenomenon than before. At Zia and Santa Ana pueblos, developments began with Puname Polychrome, which resembled the last of the Rio Grande glazes. It was characterized by widely spaced and thickened elements, such as feathers, which suggested a relation to Ashiwi Polychrome, another reflection of the exchange of ideas resulting from the stress of the Spanish Conquest period. Elements on Ashiwi Polychrome were created in solid black or black outlines filled with red on a white- to a cream-colored background. The area below the bulging mid-section was slipped red or, in later examples, a red band separated the upper section from the polished but unslipped base.

By 1750, the vessel form became symmetrically globular, but remnants of the field distinction created by the mid-section bulge were continued by the separation of decora-

FIGURE 158

PUNAME POLYCHROME. *Ca. 1680–1740. Height 24.2 cm. Diameter 30.5 cm. School of American Research, Santa Fe, N. Mex. Indian Arts Fund. IAF 2156. This vessel retains the shoulder bulge so characteristic of Hawikuh ceramics. The use of the feather motif is associated both with prayer and rain in Pueblo mythology. (See appendix, p. 143)*

tions into bands. Sweeping curved elements were present in the lower band, while the feather motifs on the upper section became rounded and more stylized. Representations of clouds, seed pods, and the use of negative structures within motifs came into use on Trios Polychrome. As this type began to change to Zia Polychrome, the vessel form took on a contracting lower segment and the maximum diameter moved upward. Naturalistic birds and flowers began to appear, and red elements were often without black outlines.

The first Spanish settlement occurred about the same time as Tewa Polychrome. It has been suggested that the use of red might have been influenced by the Spanish or by the Mexican Indians who accompanied Oñate in 1598. An alternative explanation is that northern potters at this time began to borrow the idea of a red slip from

FIGURE 159

Top:
Fig. 159. ASHIWI POLYCHROME. Ca. 1700–1750. Height 12.5 cm. Diameter 21.5 cm. Museum of the American Indian, Heye Foundation, N.Y. Collected by George H. Pepper, 6/6370. Although this jar illustrates the return to a matte paint, its form retains many attributes from the earlier Hawikuh Polychrome. The use of a concave base was introduced to Zuñi ceramics at this time.

Bottom right:
Fig. 161. SAN PABLO POLYCHROME. Ca. 1740–1800. Height 32.5 cm. Diameter 32.5 cm. Fred Harvey Collection, The Heard Museum, Phoenix, Ariz. 112-P. The symmetrical globular shape of this jar is one attribute that separates the type from Puname Polychrome. Its motifs continue the stylized treatment of biomorphic units such as plants and bird parts, while the lower sweeping festoon lines are from decorations on late Rio Grande glazes.

FIGURE 160

SAN PABLO POLYCHROME. *Ca. 1740–1800. Height 22.9 cm. Diameter 27.9 cm. School of American Research, Santa Fe, N. Mex. Indian Arts Fund. IAF 84. Attributes from both the late Rio Grande glazes and Ashiwi Polychrome are characteristic of this type. Stylized feathers are an important part of the design.*

FIGURE 161

other Pueblo peoples who were then making glaze decorated wares. Some reinforcement may have come from the Ácoma people who had been brought to the Rio Grande region by Zaldivar. Whatever the origin, Tewa Polychrome was characterized by a heavy red slip on both the upper and lower areas of jars. The two zones were divided by a white-slipped band that corresponded to the bulging area of the vessel wall. On the white band, simple narrow line decorations were drawn. Most common were sets of two or three parallel zigzag lines that were sometimes separated by dots. In all cases the line-work was relatively crude. Bowls had designs of the same form on a white band that formed the rim area; a keel divided the decorated band from the red under-body. Only in the late pieces of Tewa Polychrome that were made near the time of the Pueblo Rebellion were there design adaptations from Spanish ceramics and modified European vessel shapes.[93]

From 1750 to 1875, the earlier widespread styles began to give way to ceramics distinctive of various pueblos. Differences were relatively suggestive of varieties, however, and many attributes still crosscut larger groupings. Not all pieces can be assigned to one pueblo or another with certainty. Nevertheless, the germ of specialization that marks the Modern period began to be present and seems to duplicate trends that took place in earlier periods of Pueblo history. In each case, the products were the results of unique events from population realignments after periods of stress.

In general, surviving pieces included jar bodies of a globular shape with a general lack of structural differentiation between the upper and lower body sections. Necks, although different in contour, tended to be low. Bowls mimicked the shape of the lower three-fifths of jars but exhibited a slightly flaring rim. A white slip covered the upper three-fourths of the jars and the upper half of bowls. Designs were executed in black carbon paint on the white slip. Between the white-slipped section and the under-body was a red band. An all-over red slip was found in some instances, and on these, the black decorations were applied onto the red background in the same area of the vessel and in the same style as on the polychromes.

FIGURE 162

POWHOGE POLYCHROME. *Ca. 1750–1820. Height 44 cm. Diameter 45.7 cm. From the Collection of Mr. and Mrs. Larry Frank, Arroyo Hondo, N. Mex. Unlike earlier examples, the decorative field on this jar was not divided, and heavy figures were used instead of fine-line flower or feather-like patterns.*

This general style was found from the Rio Grande Keresan pueblos northward throughout most of the Tewa pueblos. Although it probably came into existence among the Tewas as Powhoge Polychrome and Powhoge Black-on-red, it spread southward rapidly. Appearance of the form in the south happened at about the time that manufacture of glaze ware ceased. San Felipe apparently stopped making decorated pottery at this time, but Santo Domingo and Cochiti became important centers.

The criteria by which one can distinguish vessels made at one pueblo from those made at the other appear after about 1820. By the beginning of the Modern period, it is possible to identify Cochiti Polychrome and Santo Domingo Polychrome as distinct types. In the Tewa area, only the pueblos of San Ildefonso, Tesuque, and Nambe appeared to be involved in a major way with the subsequent development of polychrome wares; San Juan and Santa Clara seemed to drop decoration in favor of polished wares that continued the older Tewa vessel shape.

There is an interesting relationship between a number of types grouped into the Tewa Gray, Black, and Red wares and the evolution of many ceramics being made today in the northern Rio Grande region. Vessels classified within the wares seem to have served a multitude of functions ranging from general household activities to specific ceremonial purposes.

The Protohistoric and Historic periods manifest the important effect of the exchange of ideas on ceramic traditions. In the Prehistoric period, one can see the reasonably precise spatial boundaries that can be drawn around discrete ceramic traditions. In the Protohistoric and Historic periods, a sense of the manner in which these boundaries arose and were modified can be reached.

In every area there were native inhabitants and there were migrants. The migrations were the result of major political and cultural disruptions that affected the area. While the movements might have been brief, they had lasting effects. Some of the migrants chose to stay, and if they were potters, they had a lasting effect on the local pottery tradition. But even more importantly, those individuals who remained in an alien land for only a short period before returning home generated perhaps the greatest change — when they brought new ideas to their hosts, and when they returned to their birthplace with innovative ideas. It is undoubtedly through similar movements, of which we have only the palest evidence, that the strong traditions of the Prehistoric period were established, sustained, and modified.

Similarly, the potters of the Protohistoric and Historic periods borrowed from the past. The use of the past, then, is not a simple effort on the part of modern artists to capture the tourist market. It is a recurrent theme in Puebloan craftsmanship. Prehistoric sites were both libraries and laboratories of ceramic practice, and they were apparently revisited periodically. The motivation for the revival of older traditions must remain a matter of speculation, but one could guess that the symbols of previous generations were powerful weapons in the hands of more conservative members of a group who wished to stress the value of tradition and the correctness of the past.

Generations in Clay: Conclusion

IN THE PRECEDING CHAPTERS, an attempt has been made to set forth the major directions of Pueblo art in ceramics. Beginning with the Modern period and working through the Prehistoric, Protohistoric, and Historic periods, a number of trends have been identified. Plainwares, bichromes, and polychromes are still made in various Pueblo communities. Using the archaeological record of the past, it is known that plainwares were first made about 1,800 years ago, bichromes about 1,400 years ago, and polychromes about 1,000 years ago. Design statements from this past are as valid today as they were then.

With the existence of an adequate written record from

the last 100 years, it is possible to identify the villages in which particular vessels and art styles have been made and continue to be produced today. The individuals involved in their manufacture and the events that shaped the growth of the craft are known to us. Thus, the Modern period provides many of our best insights to the dynamics of Pueblo ceramic art. For example, we can easily appreciate the effect of what was seen in prehistoric sherds from Awatovi on the work of the Hopi potter Nampeyo, or of sherds from the Pajarito Plateau on the work of Maria Martinez, or those from the Ácoma region on pottery made by Lucy Lewis. The incorporation of old designs into a new interpretation is a phenomenon that almost certainly occurred hundreds of times in the prehistoric past.

The "regressive" tendencies that archaeologists identify in the pottery of the Prehistoric period often may have been viewed by the artisans of those times as an important reaffirmation of their past. We can only guess as to how often these artisans were at the forefront of a religious revival or a traditional political movement.

There are obvious difficulties in reconstructing the emotional aspects of aesthetics for populations of the past without written records, but certain assumptions permit conjecture based on logic and objective criteria. The fact that Pueblo people have continued to decorate ceramics for at least 1,400 years indicates that value was accorded to that procedure. Polishing, decoration, and other manipulations required extra time that could have been spent in more practical, life-supporting activities. Existing evidence indicates that the decoration of ceramics played an important role in group identity, boundary maintenance, and the rela-

tion of people to their environment — physical and spiritual — whereby elements of the world can exist in harmony. In the past, when social interaction both within and between Pueblo communities existed at a high level, artistic activity was greatest. Often, this interaction was accompanied by an intensification of religious phenomena, and vital symbols were incorporated into all of Pueblo art.

Today, only a few ceramic pieces continue to play a role in Pueblo society; ceremonial and funerary usages are two such functions. This has led Pueblo artists to respond to outside values, since most of their products must find an economic outlet. The various fairs, shows, and competitions are usually judged not by Pueblo Indians but by others who represent the "market." The innovations by Pueblo artists based on traditional representations have found an aesthetic appeal within the concepts of the purchasing groups. The particular uniqueness and individuality of Pueblo pottery is an escape from the monotonous sameness of mass production. Moreover, it recalls a cultural past of great beauty. The status of even the best modern pieces made before World War II has now changed from that of a curio item to a decorative art, both in terms of appreciation and monetary value. Beyond these economic factors, however, Pueblo potters today express their feelings in the enjoyment they obtain by making objects that others enjoy. The direction of this creativity is not random; it exists within the framework of tradition.

Over many generations, Pueblo ceramic artisans have drawn on a continually growing body of knowledge and experience. Today, much of what appears as new is actually the old, used in different contexts and in different ways.

Appendix

This appendix lists the principle Southwestern pottery wares and types treated in this book. When a type has been described or illustrated in the text, reference is made to the page on which it is found. When a description has not been provided in the text, it appears in brief form in this appendix. Contemporary, village-specific ceramics are not included in this appendix.

UPPER SAN JUAN BROWN WARE
1. Los Pinos Brown (text p. 74), A.D. 1–400
2. Sambrito Brown (text p. 74)
3. Rosa Brown (text p. 74), A.D. 700–950

TUSAYAN GRAY WARE
1. Lino Gray (text p. 74)
2. Obelisk Gray (text p. 74)
3. Lino Black-on-gray (text p. 77), A.D. 550–875

TUSAYAN WHITE WARE
1. Kana-a Black-on-white (text p. 77, ill. p. 78)
2. Black Mesa Black-on-white (text p. 78, ill. pp. 78, 79)
3. Sosi Black-on-white (text p. 78, ill. p. 79)
4. Dogoszhi Black-on-white (text p. 79, ill. p. 80)
5. Polacca Black-on-white (text p. 79), A.D. 1250–1300
6. Flagstaff Black-on-white (text p. 79, ill. p. 80)
7. Kayenta Black-on-white (text p. 81, ill. p. 80)
8. Wupatki Black-on-white (text p. 81), A.D. 1125–1300
9. Betatakin Black-on-white (text and ill. p. 81)
10. Tusayan Black-on-white (ill. p. 81), A.D. 1150–1300. A variant of Kayenta Black-on-white.
11. Hovapi Black-on-white, A.D. 1250–1300. A variant of Kayenta Black-on-white.
12. Bidahochi Black-on-white (text p. 81, ill. p. 82), A.D. 1300–1400. It appears that this type was a speciality ware within a very limited part of the region. In concept, the design was identical to that of early Jeddito Black-on-yellow, with which it was contemporaneous. The negative style was again open, so that massed solids were less evident and lines became narrower. Crosshatching and filled, stepped spaces were used, suggesting a heritage from previous types.

CIBOLA WHITE WARE
1. La Plata Black-on-white (text p. 85, ill. p. 83)
2. White Mound Black-on-white (text p. 85), A.D. 700–800. This type retained some design elements from La Plata Black-on-white, but they were reorganized into more complicated patterns, which included checkerboards within bands; bands made up of several parallel lines in a zigzag pattern, sometimes bounded by a line with pendant triangles; negative squares and diamonds; and outlined motifs composed of plain, ticked, or saw-tooth-edged triangles. Designs that built up from a circle in the bottom of a bowl were uncommon, and isolated motifs were rare. Late forms had many parallels with Mogollon Red-on-brown from the south (Gladwin 1945: plate 11, 22–23; Wendorf 1953: fig. 74).
3. Kiatuthlanna Black-on-white (text p. 85), A.D. 800–870. This

type succeeded White Mound Black-on-white in many parts of the region. It was mostly a transitional type and is infrequently found as the dominant representative at a site (Weaver 1978: 124–125). It has been described as having a clean, clear white background; hard polished surface; and dense black paint (Gladwin 1945: plate 22). At least three major styles evolved in addition to a continuation of designs from White Mound Black-on-white. One was similar to Piedra Black-on-white: groups of fine parallel lines extended in a zigzag or geometric pattern and lines often crossed at the corners forming rectangular units; diagonal lines were drawn in these, resulting in triangular spaces that were filled in, forming opposed solids; the triangles had ticked edges, and cross-ticking was sometimes found between opposed figures. The second style consisted of wavy line-hatching of curvilinear or rectilinear forms and was similar in layout to the previous style. Some curvilinear figures ended in an interlocking scroll. The third style consisted of bands of interlocking scrolls rising from solid triangles with ticked edges. The scroll was almost identical to examples on the earlier Hohokam type, Santa Cruz Red-on-buff.

4. Red Mesa Black-on-white (text p. 85), A.D. 870–950. Development of this type involved many variations in the use of local clays, tempers, and minor style differences — for example, the unnamed variety in the Rio Grande Valley. Early examples included a slip of medium thickness. Especially in the north, however, the slip became thin, poorly polished, or not polished at all, and it was carelessly applied. Design styles remained similar to Kiatuthlanna Black-on-white but were slightly heavier. One addition was the beginning of straight line-hatching in rectilinear figures.

5. Puerco Black-on-white (text and ill. p. 85)
6. Escavada Black-on-white (text p. 85, ill. p. 84)
7. Gallup Black-on-white (text p. 85, ill. p. 84)
8. Chaco Black-on-white (text p. 86, ill. p. 85)
9. Cebolleta Black-on-white, A.D. 950–1100. This type was white-slipped, polished, and composed of sherd-tempered white paste. Some early examples had only solid elements forming motifs, which balanced the amount of painted field with unpainted areas; others copied the designs of Socorro Black-on-white (see Appendix, p. 138). Opposed hatched and solid motifs that were mirror images, rectilinear or curvilinear, became more frequent in later examples. The tendency was to imitate the styles of Wingate Black-on-red and Puerco Black-on-red that were found throughout this time. Unlike Socorro Black-on-white, this type was probably used only for trade in the Rio Grande Valley. In a local context, the interactions with the region immediately to the south resulted in many similarities to Reserve Black-on-white.

10. Reserve Black-on-white (text and ill. p. 86)
11. Tularosa Black-on-white (text p. 87, ill. p. 86)
12. Snowflake Black-on-white (text p. 87, ill. pp. 87, 88)
13. Wide Ruins Black-on-white, A.D. 1250–1300. There are still questions as to the relationships of this type, Klageto Black-on-white, and Roosevelt Black-on-white to other types. All three were contemporaneous and exhibited the balance of solid and hatched figures that became the hallmark of the period. The first two have been described from collections made along the Little Colorado River, and some design elements were derived from the Kayenta style (Colton and Hargrave 1937: 242–244, 249–250). Roosevelt Black-on-white (ill. p. 87) was found most frequently from the Mogollon Rim southward into the Roosevelt Lake district of Arizona. It is believed to be derived from Tularosa Black-on-white, but designs often resembled a complex textile (Hawley 1950: 53–54). The closest design parallel is with two late Hohokam types, Sacaton Red-on-buff and Casa Grande Red-on-buff (Zaslow and Dittert 1977b: 10–20).

LITTLE COLORADO WHITE WARES

1. St. Joseph Black-on-white (text p. 89), A.D. 700–900.
2. Holbrook A Black-on-white (text p. 90), A.D. 1075–1130
3. Holbrook B Black-on-white (text p. 90), A.D. 1075–1130
4. Padre Black-on-white (text p. 90), A.D. 1075–1200
5. Walnut Black-on-white (text and ill. p. 90)
6. Leupp Black-on-white, A.D. 1100–1200. This type was characterized by a negative design similar to Tusayan Black-on-white.

MESA VERDE WHITE WARES

1. Chapin Black-on-white (text p. 90, ill. p. 91)
2. Piedra Black-on-white (text p. 90, ill. p. 91)
3. Cortez Black-on-white (text p. 91)
4. Mancos Black-on-white (text p. 91)
5. McElmo Black-on-white (text p. 91, ill. p. 92)
6. Mesa Verde Black-on-white (text p. 91, ill. pp. 92, 94)
7. Mesa Verde Polychrome (text p. 93), A.D. 1200–1300. A variety of Mesa Verde Black-on-white, with solid figures outlined with dense mineral paint and filled with thin carbon paint (Abel 1955: Ware 10B, Type 3).

UPPER SAN JUAN WHITE WARES

1. Rosa Black-on-white (text p. 81, ill. p. 82)
2. Piedra Black-on-white (text p. 83; see also Mesa Verde White Wares, appendix p. 137), A.D. 850–950 in the Upper San Juan region.
3. Arboles Black-on-white (text p. 83, ill. p. 82)
4. Bancos Black-on-white (text p. 83), A.D. 850 and 1000. The paste of this type was a uniform white, and there was a thin slip on polished surfaces; slip color was the same as the paste, and the paint was carbon. In contrast to decorations on Piedra

Black-on-white, there was a greater use of dots, ticked lines bordering the rim, and lines with pendant triangles. Groups of narrow parallel lines, often in a zigzag pattern, as well as crosshatched motifs were direct copies of the Piedra style.

5. Gallina Black-on-white (text and ill. p. 83), A.D. 1050–1300. Most researchers have argued that this type was the subsequent one in this series (cf., Mera 1935:8), even though the greatest number of remains from the Largo-Gallina Phase have been found on the southeast side of the Continental Divide. There was a continuation of the carbon paint tradition, and designs became simplified and more widely spaced. Only a small amount of the field was painted. Designs were geometric and linear in form but generally crudely applied. Dots, groups of parallel lines, crosshatching, and checkerboard motifs were used. Isolated motifs included a solid hourglass figure, hatched triangles, and nested chevrons attached to a line (Wilkenson 1958:193; Hawley 1950:35; Hibben 1949).

6. Vallecitos Black-on-white (text p. 128), A.D. 1250–1300

7. Jemez Black-on-white (text and ill. p. 128)

EARLY RIO GRANDE WHITE WARES

1. San Marcial Black-on-white (text p. 88), A.D. 750–950. Designs employed saw-tooth elements or lines with pendant triangles as well as the beginning of checkerboard motifs and diamonds. Isolated elements or motifs in the field were not unusual, and divisions of the field were sometimes in two-fold, three-fold, or four-fold symmetry or were asymmetrical.

2. Red Mesa Black-on-white, Rio Grande variety (text and ill. p. 88)

3. Kwahe'e Black-on-white (text p. 88), A.D. 1125–1225. In terms of decoration, this type exhibited both the use of heavy solid figures and hatched areas, usually in a band layout. Solids included checkerboard motifs, opposed lines with large solid triangles, and triangles with pendant short lines; the hatched elements were often the same form as the solids. A rectilinear style was usual, but there were a few curvilinear forms. The mixing of hatched and solid figures on the same vessel was not as common as their independent occurrence; hatched elements were used more often than solids (Peckham and Reed 1963:11).

4. Taos Black-on-white (text p. 88), A.D. 1150–1250. Similar to Kwahe'e Black-on-white but with broader lines.

5. Socorro Black-on-white (text p. 88, ill. p. 89), A.D. 950–1400. The decoration on this type was placed on a highly polished but unslipped background; mineral paint was used, and the use of a sub-glaze paint increased by A.D. 1250. Changes in the designs were based largely on better execution, the use of thinner lines in hatched elements, and more complex solid figures. Basic modifications in styles were minimal. Styles included opposed solid and hatched elements, either in rectilinear or curvilinear

forms; mazes formed by parallel lines with pendant dots; bands of solid lines interrupted by checkerboard motifs; and the exclusive use of either solid geometric elements or hatched elements.

6. Chupadero Black-on-white (text and ill. p. 89)

7. Casa Colorado Black-on-white (text p. 89), A.D. 1150–1400

8. Santa Fe Black-on-white (text p. 89, ill. p. 90)

9. Wiyo Black-on-white (text and ill. p. 129)

BISCUIT WARE

1. Abiquiu Black-on-gray (text p. 130), A.D. 1375–1450

2. Bandelier Black-on-gray (text and ill. p. 129)

3. Cuyamungue Black-on-tan (text p. 129), A.D. 1450–1550

4. Sankawi Black-on-cream (text p. 129), A.D. 1500–1600

SAN JUAN RED WARES

1. Abajo Red-on-orange (text and ill. p. 95)

2. Abajo Polychrome (text p. 95), A.D. 750–850

3. Bluff Black-on-red (text p. 95), A.D. 800–900

4. Deadmans Black-on-red (text p. 95, ill. p. 96)

5. Middleton Black-on-red, A.D. 1050–1130. An unpainted variety, Middleton Red, appears to have been made north and west of the Colorado River in extreme northern Arizona and adjacent Utah. The decorative style of the painted type was confined to hatched panels. Solid areas characteristic of the earlier Deadmans Black-on-white were not used.

6. Nankoweap Polychrome, A.D. 1125–1160. Decorations were black and red on orange, similar to Citadel Polychrome. The two were distinct in that Citadel Polychrome utilized crushed sherd temper and, in this type, only sand temper was used.

7. Amusovi Polychrome, A.D. 1250–1300. Styles on this type were like Kayenta Polychrome, with decorations painted in a combination of dull red, black, and white. The sherd temper of Kayenta Polychrome was not found in this type. Instead, it was characterized by sand and crushed rock temper.

8. Machonpi Polychrome, A.D. 1250. The decorations were like Amusovi Polychrome except for the lack of black paint (Colton 1956: Ware 5A).

TSEGI ORANGE WARE

1. Medicine Black-on-red, A.D. 1075–1125. This type was decorated with solid figures and heavy lines contrasting with finer lines.

2. Tusayan Black-on-red (text and ill. p. 98), A.D. 1050–1150. Designs were hatched elements in a Dogoszhi style.

3. Tusayan Polychrome (text p. 98), A.D. 1250–1285

4. Cameron Polychrome, A.D. 1075–1150. Both orange and red were used along with hatched elements in black.

5. Citadel Polychrome (text p. 98, ill. p. 97), A.D. 1115–1200. Red stripes outlined by black on an orange background.

6. Tsegi Orange, A.D. 1200–1300. Polished orange surface without added decoration.

7. Tsegi Red-on-orange, A.D. 1225–1300. Large red areas on an orange background.
8. Tsegi Black-on-orange, A.D. 1225–1300. Narrow, parallel black lines on an orange background.
9. Tsegi Polychrome, A.D. 1225–1300. Red interior decorated with narrow black lines; exterior had red stripes on an orange background.
10. Dogoszhi Polychrome, A.D. 1250–1300. Interior designs executed in black in a Dogoszhi style; red lines used on the exterior.
11. Kayenta Polychrome, A.D. 1250–1300. Red stripes used on the exterior; the interior had a complex of black lines outlining red stripes, and white lines outlining the black and red. Black was sometimes used in a series of parallel lines or in hatching. Often, there were staggered black elements.
12. Kiet Siel Polychrome, A.D. 1225–1300. Use of black bands on red often with stepped or diagonal hatching outlined by white.
13. Kiet Siel Black-on-red, A.D. 1250–1300. Same designs as Kiet Siel Polychrome but without the white outlines.
14. Jeddito Black-on-orange, A.D. 1275–1400. Black paint was used in broad lines, diagonal hatching, solid triangles with a hook, and stepped lines.
15. Jeddito Polychrome, A.D. 1250–1300. Same designs as Jeddito Black-on-orange but white paint was used to outline black areas.
16. Klageto Black-on-yellow, A.D. 1250. Black was used for wide black stripes with parallel fine lines. Staggered lines in a series and solid elements formed by stepped figures were used.
17. Klageto Polychrome, A.D. 1250. Same as Klageto Black-on-yellow except for white diagonal stripes on the exterior surface of bowls.
18. Kintiel Black-on-orange, A.D. 1275–1300. Use of heavy black horizontal lines with parallel fine black lines. Line breaks were common, and designs exhibited a tendency toward a negative aspect in the use of staggered figures.
19. Kintiel Polychrome, A.D. 1250–1300. In addition to the motifs used on Kintiel Black-on-orange, there were white motifs on the exterior that were composed of narrow elements or, sometimes, simple depictions (Colton 1956: Ware 5B).

WINSLOW ORANGE WARE

1. Tuwiuca Orange, A.D. 1250–1300. A plain orange surface without painted decoration. The exterior surface was polished but not slipped.
2. Tuwiuca Black-on-orange, A.D. 1250–1300. Decorations consisted of a wide black stripe below the rim with a band of decoration below. The band was composed of parallel narrow lines, broad lines and stripes, panels of diagonal lines, or hatching and massed black solids.
3. Homolovi Polychrome, A.D. 1300–1400. Black elements included broad stripes, solid elements, and panels that were outlined with a narrow white line. Panels sometimes contained triangles with a hook, figures with stepped or saw-tooth edges, and zigzag lines.
4. Chavez Pass Black-on-red, A.D. 1300–1400. The characteristic elements included wide or narrow black stripes, or staggered lines and solid areas. Occasionally, elements in a band were hatched. All decorations were on the interior of bowls.
5. Chavez Pass Polychrome, A.D. 1300–1400. The decorative treatment was similar to Chavez Pass Black-on-red, except for white lines that bordered black elements. Also, white lines were sometimes found on bowl exteriors.
6. Black Axe Plain, A.D. 1250–1400. The surface was poorly polished and varied in color from shades of red to pinkish on the exterior; the interior was gray, tan, or pink. This type was not decorated.
7. Homolovi Black-on-red, A.D. 1300–1400. Decorated surfaces of this type were compacted by polishing, and a thin slip was sometimes applied. Designs on the bowl interiors consisted of stripes, fine narrow diagonal hatching in rectangular or stepped panels, wide staggered lines in series, and, occasionally, opposed triangles ending in a hook.
8. Black Axe Polychrome, A.D. 1300–1400. The designs in general are like Homolovi Black-on-red, but there is the use of narrow white lines to border the black stripes or panels. Only rarely were designs painted on the bowl exteriors.

JEDDITO YELLOW WARES

1. Huckovi Polychrome, A.D. 1275–1325. Designs were executed in a style similar to Kayenta Polychrome; the difference was in the use of a Hopi yellow clay. White paint was used to outline the black paint motifs.
2. Huckovi Black-on-orange, A.D. 1275–1325. The black designs were geometric, with a wide line below the rim followed by narrow parallel lines, stepped rectangles, and checkerboard motifs.
3. Kokop Polychrome, A.D. 1250–1325. Again, the designs were geometric and resembled Kayenta Polychrome but were on a Hopi yellow paste.
4. Jeddito Black-on-yellow (text and ill. 109)
5. Jeddito Stippled, A.D. 1350–1600. Identical to Jeddito Black-on-yellow except that stippling was used to fill large areas of the design.
6. Jeddito Engraved, A.D. 1350–1600. Identical to Jeddito Black-on-yellow except that geometric designs were engraved over the painted area.
7. Sikyatki Polychrome (text p. 109, ill. pp. 110, 111)
8. Awatovi Polychrome, A.D. 1400–1625. Stippling and engraving on Sikyatki design and the addition of red.
9. Kawaioku Polychrome, A.D. 1400–1625. Use of white rather

than red to form masses.

10. San Bernardo Black-on-yellow, 1628–1680. Basically derived from Jeddito Black-on-yellow and Awatovi Polychrome but showed a deterioration in the execution of designs. Early pieces were almost indistinguishable from their predecessors, but as the style developed they became cruder and heavier.

11. San Bernardo Polychrome (ill. p. 112)

12. Payupki Polychrome (text p. 131)

13. Polacca Polychrome (ill. p. 36), 1800–1900. The type included vessels with arabesque designs; life forms, clouds, and kachinas; massed black areas; massed red outlined in black; and a style that harkened back to Sikyatki Polychrome. Another variety, termed Polacca Black-on-white, lacked the use of red paint. Polacca Polychrome was distinguished from earlier ceramics by the use of a white- to buff-colored slip that was usually crazed, and the bowl forms had out-flared rims (Colton 1956: Ware 7B — Type 17; Harlow 1967:42–43; Frank and Harlow 1974: 150–151).

14. Walpi Polychrome (ill. pp. 36, 37), 1800 to present. This type is an example of traditional ceramics still manufactured for domestic use as well as for sale. With its plain yellow counterpart, the two types are said to be used especially for mutton stew. The main attribute that separates the type from Polacca Polychrome is the lack of a slip; additionally, both the red and the black paints have a brownish hue. In terms of decorative features, there are more parallels with Polacca Polychrome than differences. Late examples of Walpi Polychrome exhibit very naturalistic zoomorphic forms.

15. Walpi Black-on-yellow, 1800 to present

16. Hano Black-on-yellow (ill. p. 33)

17. Hano Polychrome (text p. 31, ill. p. 32)

WHITE MOUNTAIN RED WARE

1. Puerco Black-on-red (text and ill. p. 99), A.D. 1000–1200. These vessels were generally decorated with Sosi and earlier Tusayan design styles.

2. Wingate Black-on-red (text p. 102, ill. p. 100), A.D. 1050–1200. The Wingate designs approximate Reserve and Tularosa styles.

3. Wingate Polychrome (text p. 102), A.D. 1125–1200. Vessels have a black-on-red interior and either a red-on-unslipped-red or red-on-white exterior.

4. St. Johns Black-on-red (ill. p. 102), A.D. 1175–1300. Similar to Wingate Black-on-red, except for a more orange, less deep red, surface color.

5. St. Johns Polychrome (text p. 102), A.D. 1175–1300. Black-on-red interior, white-on-red exterior. St. Johns Polychrome was one of the most widely distributed ceramic types in the prehistoric Southwest. Many later polychromes were derived from its technological and design characteristics.

6. Springerville Polychrome, A.D. 1250–1300. Like St. Johns Polychrome, except for black and white on exterior.

7. Pinedale Polychrome (text p. 102), A.D. 1275–1325. Black-on-red motifs outlined in white on interior and/or exterior surface.

8. Pinedale Black-on-red (text p. 102), A.D. 1275–1325. Similar to Wingate, but approaching a Flagstaff style. Use of stylized birds.

9. Cedar Creek Polychrome (text p. 102), A.D. 1300–1375. A transitional design style between Pinedale and Four Mile Polychrome.

10. Four Mile Polychrome (text p. 102, ill. p. 103), A.D. 1300–1400. Black and white-on-red interiors and exteriors. White was used as a framing line for black designs.

11. Showlow Polychrome (text p. 102, ill. p. 106), A.D. 1325–1400. Use of black and red on a white background over some portion of the vessel surface.

12. Kinishba Polychrome (text p. 102, ill. p. 105), A.D. 1300–1350

13. Point of Pines Polychrome (text p. 102), A.D. 1400–1450. Similar to Four Mile Polychrome but with tuff and mica temper.

RIO GRANDE GLAZE A

1. Los Padillas Glaze-polychrome (text p. 124), A.D. 1300–1350

2. Agua Fria Glaze-on-red (text p. 124, ill. p. 126)

3. Arenal Glaze Polychrome, A.D. 1350–1400. The exteriors of bowls were decorated with narrow white lines.

4. Cieneguilla Glaze-on-yellow, A.D. 1350–1425. The surface was slipped with a whitish to light-yellow clay, rather than red.

5. Cieneguilla Glaze Polychrome, A.D. 1350–1425. Also had a yellow slip, but some glaze-outlined elements were red-filled.

6. Sanchez Glaze-on-red, A.D. 1350–1425. Agua Fria Glaze-on-red with an everted rim.

7. Sanchez Glaze-on-yellow, A.D. 1350–1425. Cieneguilla Glaze-on-yellow with an everted rim.

8. Sanchez Glaze Polychrome, A.D. 1350–1425. San Clemente Glaze Polychrome with an everted rim.

9. San Clemente Glaze Polychrome, A.D. 1350–1425. Characterized by contrasting slip colors on the bowl interior and exterior: the interior was a light yellow to white while the exterior was red.

10. Pottery Mound Glaze-polychrome (text p. 126), A.D. 1350–1500. Utilized red-filled elements, and the design style resembled that of Sikyatki Polychrome (Eighth Southwestern Ceramic Seminar 1966).

RIO GRANDE GLAZE B

1. Largo Glaze-on-yellow, A.D. 1400–1475

2. Largo Glaze Polychrome (ill. p. 126), A.D. 1425–75. Differed from Largo Glaze-on-yellow in the use of multiple colors.

3. Largo Glaze-on-red, A.D. 1425–1475. Red rather than yellow background.

4. Medio Glaze Polychrome, A.D. 1425–1475. Contrasting slips on

the two surfaces of bowls were similar to San Clemente Glaze Polychrome.

RIO GRANDE GLAZE C
1. Espinosa Glaze-polychrome (text p. 126, ill. p. 125)

RIO GRANDE GLAZE D
1. San Lazaro Glaze Polychrome (ill. p. 127), A.D. 1490–1550. The background slip ranged from fawn to an orange or red so that there was little decoration. As a result, the high-luster glaze paint was the most obvious feature. Designs were still in bands, but there were all-over patterns with birds, keys, zigzags, and oblique lines. Decorations were as common on the exterior of bowls as on the interior. In addition to the dark slip, the rim form was also a distinguishing feature. The rims were high and tapered, and the interior surface was gently convex; the exterior was straight to slightly recurved, and the shoulder became a common part of the bowl form. (Hawley 1950:85–86; Eighth Southwestern Ceramic Seminar 1966.)

RIO GRANDE GLAZE E
1. Puaray Glaze Polychrome, A.D. 1500–1600
2. Escondido Glaze Polychrome, A.D. 1515–1650. This type had an all-over light background and sometimes had a red slip on the exterior surface of bowls. The rim often copied the contemporary black-on-white types found north of La Bajada Hill.
3. Pecos Glaze Polychrome, A.D. 1515–1650. This type probably was made at Pecos Pueblo, east of Santa Fe, New Mexico. Distinctive attributes were the use of sand temper instead of crushed rock found in the other types and a rim shape on bowls that has been described as looking like a "fat comma."

RIO GRANDE GLAZE F
1. Encierro Glaze Polychrome, 1650–1750. A brownish-black or dark brown thick, runny paint was used. Bowl rims were elongated and served as a decorated zone.
2. Kotyiti Glaze-on-yellow, 1650–1750. This type had a white to light-yellow slip that either covered both surfaces, or covered all but the area below the rim on the exterior of bowls. In the latter instance, the lower exterior wall was not slipped.
3. Kotyiti Glaze-on-red, 1650–1750. The same conditions pertained as with Kotyiti Glaze-on-yellow except that the slip was a streaked red color. The two polychromes had both white and red slips; red elements in the design were rare. Forms that were found in all of the types include shouldered bowls, bowls with an angle between the rim and the body, jars with a bulging midsection and concave base, cups, and soup plates (Hawley 1950: 88–89; Eighth Southwestern Ceramic Seminar 1966).
4. Cicuyi Glaze Polychrome, 1650–1750. Both white and red slip.

LATER RIO GRANDE BICHROME WARE
1. Galisteo Black-on-white (text p. 129)

2. Poge Black-on-white, A.D. 1325–1350. This type was a localized development from Galisteo Black-on-white. Characteristically, it had a soft thin slip, and while the designs follow Galisteo Black-on-white, the line-work was much poorer. Stubbs and Stallings (1953:56) suggest that the type may have represented the spread of Towa-speaking people in the crescent from Jemez to Pecos Pueblo.
3. Sakona Black-on-tan, 1580–1650. This type and Sakona Polychrome formed the bridge between ceramics decorated only with black carbon paint and polychromes where red was used to slip the under-body. The interiors of bowls were divided into panels embellished with a diagonal line. The bowl form was marked by a sharp, angular keel between the rim segment and the lower body. The red under-body was added about A.D. 1650 (Harlow 1973:28).
4. Powhoge Black-on-red (text p. 133), 1830–1850

LATER RIO GRANDE PLAIN WARE
1. Potsuwi'i Incised (text p. 70), A.D. 1425–1550
2. Potsuwi'i Gray, A.D. 1450–1650. This type was contemporaneous in part with Potsuwi'i Incised and duplicated its shape and paste qualities but lacked the incised lines.
3. Kapo Gray, 1650–1725. Shape changes of Potsuwi'i Incised and Potsuwi'i Gray, termed Kapo Gray, followed those of the contemporary types, and, by 1650, resembled that of Sakona Polychrome.
4. Kapo Black, 1720–1800. This type was the same as Kapo Gray except for its red slip, which was then smudged to produce a lustrous black. As a standardized form, it was a short-lived type, because as other villages took up the manufacture of this style, there were local modifications in the shape.

LATER RIO GRANDE POLYCHROME WARES
1. Gobernador Polychrome (text and ill. p. 130)
2. Kiua Polychrome (text p. 54, ill. pp. 55, 56), 1775–1900. Although this type was similar to Powhoge Polychrome, Harlow (1973:48) sets forth a number of attributes by which the two may be separated. This type had an orange paste with crushed crystalline rock temper, in contrast to the tuff temper and gray to tan paste of Powhoge Polychrome. A denser black paint was also used, as well as a hard slip that, while crazed, was not well polished. The designs were formal, geometric, and paneled, and no red was used. The red band below the design was wide and relatively orange in color.
3. Sakona Polychrome (see Sakona Black-on-tan, appendix p. 141)
4. Tewa Polychrome (text p. 131), 1650–1725
5. Pojoaque Polychrome, 1700–1750. Shortly after the Spanish reconquest, Tewa Polychrome gave way to this type. The most obvious difference was the use of heavier solid elements and the

white band divided into panels. The solid elements were combined into long curved figures with pendant solid triangles, solid triangles pendant to oblique lines, and stylized feather motifs. On the lower body, a red band divided the white decorated area from the remainder of the under-body.

6. Ogapoge Polychrome, 1725–1800. This type was contemporaneous with Pojoaque Polychrome. Although it had many similarities to Tewa Polychrome, the organization of the decorated field and the designs were much closer to Sakona Polychrome. The problem in relating Ogapoge Polychrome to Sakona Polychrome is our present understanding of the time span between them. Early forms of Ogapoge Polychrome possessed the convex bulge in the jar body just below mid-height but, in later pieces, the bulge gave way to a sharply rounded shoulder. Characteristically, the area above the bulge or shoulder was slipped white. The decoration was applied to the upper part of the vessel, and motifs included large rosettes, stylized feathers resembling Ashiwi Polychrome motifs, hourglass elements with appended paint-like figures, or plant-like designs extending upward from the lower framing lines. A red band separates the under-body from the decorated area.

7. Powhoge Polychrome (text and ill. p. 133)
8. Tatungue Polychrome (text p. 57)
9. Tunyo Polychrome (ill. p. 67), 1900–1920
10. Puname Polychrome (text and ill. p. 131), 1680–1740. Design elements were created in solid black or red outlined in black on a white- to cream-colored background. The area below the bulging mid-section was slipped red or, in later examples, a red band separated the upper section from the polished but unslipped base. By 1750, the vessel form became symmetrically globular, but remnants of the field distinction that had been created by the mid-section bulge continued in the separation of decorations into bands. Sweeping curved elements were present in the lower band, while the feather motifs on the upper section became rounded and more stylized.
11. San Pablo Polychrome (ill. p. 132), 1740–1800. A derivative of Puname Polychrome at Zia Pueblo.
12. Trios Polychrome (text p. 131), 1775–1875
13. Ranchitos Polychrome, 1760–1825. A derivative of Puname Polychrome made at Santa Ana Pueblo.
14. Zia Polychrome (text p. 50, ill. pp. 49–52), 1875 to present
15. Santa Ana Polychrome (text p. 51, ill. pp. 53, 54), 1850 to present

ZUÑI WARES

1. Heshotauthla Polychrome (text p. 118), A.D. 1275 or 1300–1400. Like St. Johns Polychrome and the transition type with glaze paint, Heshotauthla Polychrome had a red to orange-red background slip. Bowl interiors were decorated with black to greenish glaze, while thin white lines were painted on the exterior, sometimes in combination with black glaze lines. Interior designs were not as well executed as St. Johns Polychrome and displayed certain changes. The curvilinear motifs were lacking, hatching became rare, and overall interior decoration was not used. Units resembling textiles were found on bowls with a quartered layout. An open appearance due to a large amount of background was a characteristic feature. Some vessels had no white elements and are referred to as Heshotauthla Black-on-red (ill. p. 112) (Woodbury and Woodbury 1966:304–310).

2. Kwakina Polychrome (ill. p. 114), A.D. 1325–1400. This type was similar to Showlow Polychrome of the White Mountain Red Ware and the Pinto-Gila-Tonto polychrome group from the Salado region. The white interior may have come into use as a result of ceramic trade or by the actual movement of peoples from the south into the Zuñi region. Unlike the Pinto-Gila-Tonto polychrome group, thin white line decoration remained on the exteriors of bowls and glaze paint was applied to the white interior background. Designs rarely filled the field, but decorative bands were often divided into oblique panels with large interlocking triangular zones. Parallel lines, stepped lines, checkerboards, pendant triangles, interlocking keys, dots pendant from lines, and negative circles in solid black triangles were common elements (Woodbury and Woodbury 1966: 311–313).

3. Pinnawa Glaze-on-white (ill. p. 115), A.D. 1350–1450. Designs were simpler than those of Kwakina and were composed of isolated elements such as paired stepped triangles, a scroll, or a stepped line on the exterior of a bowl. Sometimes the exteriors had a continuous band of a rectilinear meander or horizontal parallel lines. Interiors were decorated with a broad band of stepped triangles, oblique panels, interlocking scrolls, or checkerboard motifs with dots, or they had a sectioned layout with alternating decorated and undecorated areas. Occasionally, motifs included stylized birds at the apices of triangles. Surface designs on jars were similar to those on bowl interiors (Woodbury and Woodbury 1966:315–319).

4. Pinnawa Red-on-white, A.D. 1350–1450. Contemporary with Pinnawa Glaze-on-white. On this type, a matte red paint replaced the glaze. Designs were simpler than on Pinnawa Glaze-on-white, and interior decoration on bowls was rare. Some of the band designs found on jars appear to have been copied elements from Gila Polychrome, and there was a distinct relation to Kechipawan Polychrome.

5. Kechipawan Polychrome (text p. 118, ill. p. 117), A.D. 1375–1425. Like Pinnawa Red-on-white, this type had both the matte red and glaze paint on the white slip background, and the main field of decoration was on bowl interiors or jar exteriors. Bowl exteriors usually had only a simple encircling connected meander or only isolated elements where red was outlined by glaze lines.

Bowl interiors usually had a broad band decorated with geometric elements, stylized birds, feathers, animals, or crude human figures. The forms were created by glaze paint, and red was used to fill in areas (Woodbury and Woodbury 1966: 319–324).

6. Matsaki Polychrome (text and ill. p. 123)
7. Hawikuh Polychrome (text p. 118, ill. p. 116)
8. Ashiwi Polychrome (text p. 131, ill. p. 132)
9. Kiapkwa Polychrome (text and ill. p. 118)
10. Zuñi Polychrome (text p. 40, ill. pp. 39, 41)

ÁCOMA WARES

1. Kwakina Polychrome, A.D. 1325–1400. Like the Zuñi type (see appendix p. 142), the Ácoma bowls had a white slip on the interior with designs in a black to green glaze paint. The exterior slip was a burgundy color rather than the orange-red of the Zuñi type. Another difference was that the white paint designs on the bowl exteriors were not done at Zuñi and, when there was a decoration, the elements were drawn with glaze paint. There is some reason to believe that the style lasted longer at Ácoma than at Zuñi, and on later examples the burgundy slip moved onto the inner lip of the bowls.
2. Pinnawa Glaze-on-white, A.D. 1350–1450. At Ácoma this type was almost indistinguishable from its Zuñi counterpart (see appendix p. 142); a whiter paste appeared to be characteristic.
3. Kechipawan Polychrome, A.D. 1375–1425. This type differed from that at Zuñi (see appendix p. 142) only by a whiter paste and fewer instances of unbounded red elements. Red pigments

used at Ácoma had a slight purple hue when compared with the Zuñi examples.
4. Hawikuh Polychrome (text p. 122, also see appendix p. 143), 1630–1680
5. Hawikuh Glaze-on-red (text p. 122, ill. p. 120)
6. Ako Polychrome, 1700–1750. The decorations on this type were confined to the white-slipped upper body and showed a preoccupation with the feather motif; the lower body was slipped red.
7. Acomita Polychrome (text p. 122), 1750–1850. Thick lines were used along with dense red areas on this type, which produced a simple but bold design format. There was a gracefulness in the broad sweeping curves or scroll-like figures, which often were modifications of the previous bird forms (Frank and Harlow 1974:120).
8. McCartys Polychrome (ill. pp. 121, 122), 1850–1875. Continued reduction in the distinction between the body sections gradually evolved into the smooth curved outline characteristic of this type. A red slip defined the lower body, and vessel walls became thin again. Both the slip and draftsmanship were improved. More naturalistic birds and floral motifs began to replace solid curvilinear figures. The new style was one that became widespread from Ácoma to Zia for a short period. In the latter part of the 1800s, the trend toward the Modern period Ácoma Polychrome was already recognizable (Frank and Harlow 1974:121).
9. Ácoma Polychrome (text p. 43, ill. pp. 44, 45)
10. Laguna Polychrome (text p. 122, ill. p. 48)

The following objects are not in the exhibition: Figures 17, 104, 107, 141, and 158.

Notes

(See *Selected Bibliography,* page 147, for complete information)

1. Bunzel, 1933, pp. 6, 7
2. Bunzel, 1929, p. 16
3. Di Peso, 1974, pp. 48–49
4. E. Haury, 1976, p. 352
5. Dittert, *et al,* 1963
6. Shepard, 1961, pp. 16–17
7. Lambert, 1966, p. 3
8. Hill, W. W., 1937, p. 11
9. Steen, 1966, p. 56
10. Fontana, *et al,* 1962, pp. 49, 55
11. Dutton, 1966
12. Price, 1978, p. 113
13. Wobst, 1977, p. 321
14. Washburn, 1977, p. 6

15. Brody, 1977, p. 27
16. Shepard, 1961, p. 359
17. Chapman, 1936, p. 18
18. Bunzel, 1929
19. Shepard, 1961, p. 267
20. Hill, J., 1970; Longacre, 1970
21. Plog, S., 1977
22. LeBlanc, 1975; Marquardt, 1978
23. Turner and Lofgren, 1966
24. Hill, J., 1966
25. Parsons, 1939, p. 195
26. Parsons, 1939, p. 183
27. Tanner, 1975, pp. 85–109
28. Breed, 1972, pp. 44–46
29. Frisbie, 1973, pp. 231–237
30. Maxwell Museum of Anthropology, 1974, pp. 17–41
31. Harlow, 1973, pp. 268–271; Frank and Harlow, 1974, pp. 144–146
32. Frank and Harlow, 1974, p. 121
33. Tryk, 1979, pp. 21–23
34. Harlow, 1973, pp. 55–56
35. Harlow, 1973, pp. 56–57
36. Tanner, 1975, pp. 105–106
37. Harlow, 1973, pp. 49–50
38. Tanner, 1975, p. 102
39. Harlow, 1973, p. 49
40. Tanner, 1975, p. 106
41. Harlow, 1973, p. 35; Tanner, 1975, p. 108
42. Harlow, 1973, p. 41
43. Harlow, 1973, p. 41
44. Tanner, 1975, pp. 99–100
45. Maxwell Museum of Anthropology, 1974, pp. 50–78
46. Maxwell Museum of Anthropology, 1974, pp. 42–48; Tanner, 1975, p. 100
47. Harlow, 1973, pp. 35–36
48. Harlow, 1973, p. 36; Tanner, 1975, p. 98
49. Schroeder, 1964, p. 45
50. Maxwell Museum of Anthropology, 1974, pp. 85–107; Tanner, 1975, pp. 98–99
51. Maxwell Museum of Anthropology, 1974, pp. 79–84
52. Schroeder, 1964, p. 48
53. Harlow, 1973, pp. 207–209; Tanner, 1975, pp. 100–101
54. Tanner, 1975, pp. 100–101
55. Eddy, 1961, pp. 61–65; Dittert, et al, 1963, p. 11
56. Dittert, et al, 1963, pp. 9, 11
57. Hall, 1944, pp. 33–34
58. First Southwestern Ceramic Seminar, 1958
59. Hawley, 1950, pp. 32–33
60. Hawley, 1950, p. 43
61. Hawley, 1950, p. 34
62. Washburn, Dorothy K., personal communication
63. Martin and Rinaldo, 1950, pp. 502–519
64. Rinaldo and Bluhm, 1956, pp. 177–185
65. Colton, 1941, pp. 62–63
66. Breternitz, et al, 1974, pp. 29–31; Dittert, et al, 1961, p. 147
67. Abel, 1955, Ware 10B, Type 1; Breternitz, et al, 1974, pp. 41–44; Hayes, 1964, pp. 65, 67–79
68. Breternitz, et al, 1974, pp. 45–47; Hayes, 1964, pp. 69–70
69. Abel, 1955, Ware 10B, Type 3
70. Hargrave, Lyndon L., 1966, personal communication
71. Abel, 1955, Ware 5A, Type 1; Breternitz, et al, 1974, pp. 49–51
72. Breternitz, et al, 1974, pp. 57–59; Abel, 1955, Ware 5A, Type 4
73. Sixth Southwestern Ceramic Seminar, 1964
74. Breternitz, et al, 1974, pp. 61–63; Abel, 1955, Ware 5A, Type 5
75. Colton, 1956, Ware 6B
76. Colton, 1956, Ware 7B
77. Carlson, 1970
78. Plog, F., 1979, personal communication
79. Haury, Tenth Southwestern Ceramic Seminar, 1968
80. Schroeder, 1964, p. 45
81. Martin and Rinaldo, 1959
82. Mera, 1939, pp. 124–137
83. Frank and Harlow, 1974, p. 123
84. Woodbury and Woodbury, 1966, pp. 325–331
85. Hawley, 1950, p. 82; Eighth Southwestern Ceramic Seminar, 1966
86. Warren, 1968, p. 197
87. Eighth Southwestern Ceramic Seminar, 1966
88. Hawley, 1950, 86–87; Eighth Southwestern Ceramic Seminar, 1966
89. Reiter, 1938, pp. 113–154; Frank and Harlow, 1974, p. 116
90. Stubbs and Stallings, 1953, p. 50
91. Stubbs, 1950, p. 30
92. Colton, 1956, Ware 7B, Type 15; Harlow, 1967, pp. 40–41
93. Hawley, 1950, p. 91; Harlow, 1973, pp. 28–30; Frank and Harlow, 1974, Plate I, Figs. 6, 7

Glossary

The following terms from the text have been singled out because each has alternative meanings. A definition of usage in the present context is given.

APPLIQUE: Decoration or ornamentations created by the addition of clay fillets or modeled clay parts to the surface of vessels. The technique was not common on painted Pueblo pottery except for effigy forms. It has occurred frequently on Taos and Picuris micaceous wares.

ARABESQUE: A pattern of scrollwork that is often intertwined. The scrollwork employs conventionalized leaves and floral motifs.

AWANYU (Avanyu): A horned and plumed serpent representation. Also known as "kolowisi."

BAND: An encircling area of design usually bounded by horizontal framing lines. May or may not be partitioned into distinct sections or panels.

BLOCK FAULT: A dislocation of a section of the earth's crust that results from stresses. One unit is elevated relative to an adjacent unit.

CARBON PAINT (organic paint): Pigment derived from plants, often the Rocky Mountain bee plant. Plant material is soaked in water and/or boiled down to a small black cake. A dampened brush will pick up pigment from the cake. When fired in a reducing atmosphere, the carbon pigment turns black.

CERAMIC: Clay that has been altered by heating. Sufficient heat causes changes in the structure of clay minerals so that the object will not return to a plastic state when soaked in water.

COIL-AND-SCRAPE: A wall-thinning process used in making a clay vessel. Fillets of clay are coiled one upon the other, pressed together, and then scraped to obtain a uniform or desired thickness of the wall.

CURING: After raw clay is prepared by grinding, winnowing, or other procedures, it is mixed with enough water to make it plastic. Temper may or may not be added at this point. The body is set aside and kept damp for a curing period before use.

ENGRAVING: Scratching through the surface of a fired clay object to produce a decoration.

FLOATING: Polishing of an unslipped clay surface. The action brings fine particles to the surface and produces a smooth, hard layer.

GLAZE PAINT: In the Southwest, glazes were made by mixing minerals that fuse when heated. Lead oxide is usually dominant; minerals such as copper oxide, iron oxide, and manganese oxide are agents that produce colors. Native New World glazes were always decorative and were not applied as an all-over coating.

INCISING: Scratching through the surface of a clay wall while the clay is still damp to produce decorations.

KEEL: The point where a sharp convex angular change in the contour of a vessel takes place.

LINE BREAK (line-gap, ceremonial break): A small interruption in the band design. It may be present only in the framing lines of the band, or the entire band design may be broken by a short gap.

MAJOLICA: A glazed and decorated soft paste pottery named for the island of Majorca (Mallorca). The pottery was made in Italy and Spain and was introduced into Mexico, where quantities were produced. Some pieces were brought to the Southwest by the Spanish.

MANO: A rectangular-shaped stone used in the mano and metate grinding set. The mano is the stone that is moved to produce the grinding action.

MATTE PAINT: A dull paint, usually a mineral or clay-based pigment that is not vitrified or glossy. On some Southwestern types, especially those from the Mogollon, there may be a polish over the matte paint.

MESA: A topographic term referring to an elevated tableland bounded by relatively vertical slopes. It is usually the result of erosion rather than an uplift of the geologic deposits.

METATE: A large stone on which the mano is moved to grind maize, seeds, clays, or other materials.

MICRO-SERIATION: Placing designs in relative chronological order by the changes that occur in the attribute state of elements within a design motif.

MODELED: Formation of a desired shape by manipulation of a piece, or pieces, of clay. An entire vessel might be modeled, or a modeled applique might be attached to a vessel wall.

MOTIF: A unit of design formed by a combination of elements. The combination is usually repeated in a formal arrangement.

NEGATIVE: Said to be characteristic of a design when the amount of painted area exceeds that of the amount of visible background area.

OXIDIZING ATMOSPHERE: The condition that occurs when the fuel used to fire a clay vessel is stacked loosely so that there is more oxygen within the pyre than is being consumed in the burning of the fuel.

PADDLE-AND-ANVIL: The process of thinning a vessel wall by holding an anvil on the interior of the wall and striking the exterior with a small, flat paddle.

PANEL: As used in the description of design organization, panel refers to a division of a band. The divisions are usually accomplished by a vertical line or lines connecting the upper and lower framing lines of a band.

PLASTIC: A medium is said to be plastic when it is capable of being formed into a desired shape. Clay becomes plastic when mixed with water.

POPULATION AGGREGATION: The coming together of peoples into a relatively limited space to form a cohesive unit.

POTSHERD: One of the fragments of a broken ceramic object.

POTTERY: Earthenware; clay ware that has been formed and hardened by firing. The word has been used here as a synonym for ceramics.

REDUCING ATMOSPHERE: A condition created in firing a vessel when an excess of fuel or other means inhibits the amount of oxygen that comes into contact with the object.

RESIST: The intentional use of some means by which a portion of the vessel wall is not affected by smudging. A portion of the wall might be covered with a potsherd so that the carbon does not reach that section of the wall.

SGRAFFITO: A type of engraving accomplished after a clay object has been polished or fired. Designs are produced by removing the surface to reveal a contrasting color and the texture of the paste.

SHAKING PROCESS: The rate at which clay disintegrates when immersed in water. The rate of shaking affects the time it takes to bring clay to a plastic state.

SLIP: A slip is a fine clay applied to the surface of a vessel. Slips are used to fill pores and obtain a uniform color and smoothness. The slip color may or may not contrast with the color of the paste.

STYLE: A unique method of composition wherein distinctive combinations of elements are used.

SYMBOL: A representative depiction on the surface of a vessel.

TECHNOLOGY: Application of principles to the production of an object.

TEXTURED: Manipulation of the surface by intentional punching, impressing, incising, engraving, or other means to produce a desired pattern.

TYPE: A group of pottery vessels that are alike in every important characteristic except (possibly) shape.

WARE: A group of pottery vessels that have a majority of characteristics in common but may differ in others.

YUCCA: A plant found from the Southwest to Central America that has a long, narrow, fiberous leaf and a woody stem with bell-shaped drooping flowers. Paintbrushes are made from the leaves by native Southwestern potters.

Selected Bibliography

Abel, Leland J. 1955. "Pottery Types of the Southwest: Wares 5A, 10A, 10B, 12A." *Museum of Northern Arizona Ceramic Series* (No. 3). Flagstaff.

Breed, William J. 1972. "Hopi Bowls Collected by John Wesley Powell." *Plateau* 45 (No. 1): 44–46. Flagstaff, Ariz.

Breternitz, David A.; Rohn, Arthur H., Jr.; and Morris, Elizabeth A. 1974. "Prehistoric Ceramics of the Mesa Verde Region." *Museum of Northern Arizona Ceramic Series* (No. 5). Flagstaff.

Brody, J. J. 1977. "Mimbres Art, Sidetracked on the Trail of a Mexican Connection." *American Indian Art Magazine* 2 (No. 4): 26–31. Scottsdale, Ariz.

Bunzel, Ruth L. 1929. "The Pueblo Potter." *Columbia University Contributions to Anthropology* Vol. 3. New York, N.Y.

———. 1933. "Zuñi Texts." *Publications of the American Ethnological Society* Vol. 15. New York, N.Y.

Carlson, Roy L. 1965. "Eighteenth-Century Navajo Fortresses of the Gobernador District." *University of Colorado Series in Anthropology* (No. 10). Boulder.

———. 1970. "White Mountain Redware: A Pottery Tradition of East Central Arizona and Western New Mexico." *Anthropological Papers of the University of Arizona* (No. 19). Tucson.

Chapman, Kenneth M. 1936. "The Pottery of Santo Domingo." *Memoirs of the Laboratory of Anthropology* Vol 1. Santa Fe, N. Mex.

Chapman, Kenneth M., and Harlow, Francis H. 1970. *The Pottery of San Ildefonso Pueblo.* School of American Research, Santa Fe, N. Mex.

Colton, Harold S. 1941. "Winona and Ridge Ruin. Part II, Notes on the Technology and Taxonomy of the Pottery." *Museum of Northern Arizona Bulletin* (No. 19). Flagstaff.

———. 1955. "Pottery Types of the Southwest: Wares 8A, 8B, 9A, 9B." *Museum of Northern Arizona Ceramic Series* (No. 3). Flagstaff.

———. 1956. "Pottery Types of the Southwest: Wares 5A, 5B, 6A, 6B, 7A, 7B, 7C." *Museum of Northern Arizona Ceramic Series* (No. 3C). Flagstaff.

Colton, Harold S., and Hargrave, Lyndon L. 1937. "Handbook of Northern Arizona Pottery Wares." *Museum of Northern Arizona Bulletin* (No. 11). Flagstaff.

d'Azevedo, Warren L. 1958. "A Structural Approach to Esthetics: Towards a Definition of Art in Anthropology." *American Anthropologist* 60 (No. 4): 702–714. Menasha, Wis.

DiPeso, Charles C. 1974. "Casas Grandes: A Fallen Trading Center of the Gran Chichimeca." *Amerind Foundation, Inc., Series* (No. 9). Dragoon, Ariz.

Dittert, Alfred E., Jr.; Eddy, Frank W.; and Dickey, Beth L. 1963. "Evidences of Early Ceramic Phases in the Navajo Reservoir District." *El Palacio* 70 (Nos. 1–2): 5–12. Santa Fe, N. Mex.

Dittert, Alfred E., Jr.; Hester, Jim J.; and Eddy, Frank W. 1961. "An Archaeological Survey of the Navajo Reservoir District, Northwestern New Mexico." *Monograph of the School of American Research* (No. 23). Santa Fe, N. Mex.

Dittert, Alfred E., Jr., and Ruppe, Reynold J. 1951. "The Archaeology of Cebolleta Mesa: A Preliminary Report." *El Palacio* 58 (No. 4): 116–129. Santa Fe, N. Mex.

Dutton, Bertha P. 1966. "Pots Pose Problems." *El Palacio* 73 (No. 1): 5–15. Santa Fe, N. Mex.

Eddy, Frank W. 1961. "Excavations at Los Pinos Phase Sites in the Navajo Reservoir District." *Museum of New Mexico Papers in Anthropology* (No. 4). Santa Fe.

Fontana, Bernard L.; Robinson, William J.; Cormack, Charles W.; and Leavitt, Ernest E., Jr. 1962. *Papago Indian Pottery*. American Ethnological Society. University of Washington Press, Seattle.

Frank, Larry, and Harlow, Francis H. 1974. *Historic Pottery of the Pueblo Indians, 1600–1880*. New York Graphic Society, Boston, Mass.

Frisbie, Theodore R. 1973. "The Influence of J. Walter Fewkes on Nampeyo: Fact or Fancy." In: *The Changing Ways of Southwestern Indians: A Historic Perspective,* edited by Albert H. Schroeder, pp. 231–244. The Rio Grande Press, Inc., Glorieta, N. Mex.

Gladwin, Harold S. 1945. "The Chaco Branch: Excavations at White Mound and in the Red Mesa Valley." *Medallion Papers* (No. 33). Globe, Ariz.

Hall, Edward T., Jr. 1944. "Early Stockaded Settlements in the Gobernador, New Mexico." *Columbia Studies in Archaeology and Ethnology* 2, Part 1. New York, N.Y.

Harlow, Francis H. 1967. *Historic Pueblo Indian Pottery*. The Monitor Press, Los Alamos, N. Mex.

———. 1973. *Matte-Paint Pottery of the Tewa, Keres, and Zuñi Pueblos*. Museum of New Mexico, Santa Fe.

Haury, Emil W. 1976. *The Hohokam: Desert Farmers and Craftsmen; Excavations at Snaketown, 1964–1965*. University of Arizona Press, Tucson.

Hawley, Florence M. 1950. "Field Manual of Prehistoric Pottery Types," rev. ed. *University of New Mexico Bulletin, Anthropological Series* Vol. 1 (No. 4). Albuquerque.

Hayes, Alden D. 1964. "The Archaeological Survey of Wetherill Mesa, Mesa Verde National Park, Colorado." *Archaeological Research Series* (No. 7-A). U.S.D.I. National Park Service, Wash., D.C.

Hibben, Frank C. 1949. "Pottery of the Gallina Complex." *American Antiquity* 14 (No. 3): 194–202. Menasha, Wis.

Hill, James N. 1966. "A Prehistoric Community in Eastern Arizona." *Southwestern Journal of Anthropology* 22 (No. 1): 9–30. Albuquerque, N. Mex.

———. 1970. "Broken K Pueblo: Prehistoric Social Organization in the American Southwest." *Anthropological Papers of the University of Arizona* (No. 18). Tucson.

Hill, W. W. 1937. "Navajo Pottery Manufacture." *University of New Mexico Bulletin, Anthropological Series* Vol. 2 (No. 3). Albuquerque.

Lambert, Marjorie F. 1966. *Pueblo Indian Pottery: Materials, Tools, and Techniques*. Museum of New Mexico Press, Santa Fe.

LeBlanc, Steven A. 1975. "Micro-Seriation: A Method for Fine Chronological Differentiation." *American Antiquity* 40 (No. 1): 22–38. Wash., D.C.

Lindsay, Alexander J., Jr., and Jennings, Calvin H. 1968. "Salado Red Ware Conference: Ninth Southwestern Ceramic Seminar." *Museum of Northern Arizona Ceramic Series* (No. 4). Flagstaff.

Longacre, William A. 1964. "Archaeology as Anthropology." *Science* 144: 1454–1455. Wash., D.C.

———. 1970. *Reconstructing Prehistoric Pueblo Societies*. School of American Research. University of New Mexico Press, Albuquerque.

Marquardt, William H. 1978. "Advances in Archaeological Seriation." In: *Advances in Archaeological Method and Theory,* edited by Michael B. Schiffer, Academic Press, New York, N.Y.

Martin, Paul S., and Rinaldo, John B. 1950. "Sites of the Reserve Phase, Pine Lawn Valley, Western New Mexico." *Fieldiana: Anthropology* 38 (No. 3): 403–577. Chicago, Ill.

Maxwell Museum of Anthropology. 1974. *Seven Families in Pueblo Pottery*. University of New Mexico Press, Albuquerque.

Mera, H. P. 1935. "Ceramic Clues to the Prehistory of North Central New Mexico." *Laboratory of Anthropology, Technical Series* (No. 8). Santa Fe, N. Mex.

———. 1937. "The 'Rain Bird,' A Study in Pueblo Design." *Memoirs of the Laboratory of Anthropology* Vol 2. Santa Fe, N. Mex.

———. 1939. "Style Trends of Pueblo Pottery in the Rio Grande and Little Colorado Culture Areas from the Sixteenth to the Nineteenth Century." *Memoirs of the Laboratory of Anthropology* Vol 3. Santa Fe, N. Mex.

Parsons, Elsie C. 1939. *Pueblo Indian Religion*. University of Chicago Press, Chicago, Ill.

Peckham, Stewart, and Reed, Erik K. 1963. "Three Sites Near Ranchos de Taos, New Mexico." In: *Highway Salvage Archaeology,* assembled by Stewart Peckham, 4: 1–28. Santa Fe, N. Mex.

Plog, Steve. 1977. *A Multivariate Approach to the Explanation of Ceramic Design Variation.* Ph.D. dissertation, University of Michigan, Ann Arbor.

Price, John A. 1978. *Native Studies: American and Canadian Indians.* McGraw-Hill Ryerson Limited, Toronto, Ont., Canada.

Reiter, Paul. 1938. "The Jemez Pueblo of Unshagi, New Mexico." Part II. *Monographs of the School of American Research* (No. 6). Santa Fe, N. Mex.

Rinaldo, John B., and Bluhm, Elaine A. 1956. "Late Mogollon Pottery Types of the Reserve Area." *Fieldiana: Anthropology* 36 (No. 7): 149–187. Chicago, Ill.

Schroeder, Gail D. 1964. "San Juan Pottery: Methods and Incentives." *El Palacio* 71 (No. 1): 45–51. Santa Fe, N. Mex.

Shepard, Anna O. 1961. "Ceramics for the Archaeologist." *Carnegie Institution of Washington Publication* (No. 609). Wash., D.C.

Smith, Watson. 1971. "Painted Ceramics of the Western Mound at Awatovi." *Papers of the Peabody Museum of Archaeology and Ethnology* (No. 38). Cambridge, Mass.

Southwestern Ceramic Seminar. 1958. *First Southwestern Ceramic Seminar: Cibola White Ware.* Museum of Northern Arizona, Flagstaff.

———. 1964. *Sixth Southwestern Ceramic Seminar: Black-on-Red Ceramics.* Museum of Northern Arizona, Flagstaff.

———. 1966. *Eighth Southwestern Ceramic Seminar: Rio Grande Glazes.* Museum of New Mexico, Santa Fe.

———. 1968. *Tenth Southwestern Ceramic Seminar: Hohokam Ceramics.* University of Arizona, Tucson.

Steen, Charlie R. 1966. "Excavations at Tse-Ta'a, Canyon de Chelly National Monument, Arizona." *Archaeological Research Series* (No. 9). U.S.D.I. National Park Service, Wash., D.C.

Stubbs, Stanley A. 1950. *Bird's-Eye View of the Pueblos.* University of Oklahoma Press, Norman.

Stubbs, Stanley A., and Stallings, W. S., Jr. 1953. "The Excavation of Pindi Pueblo, New Mexico." *Monograph of the School of American Research* (No. 18). Santa Fe, N. Mex.

Tanner, Clara Lee. 1975. *Southwest Indian Craft Arts* (5th printing). University of Arizona Press, Tucson.

Taylor, Donna. 1959. "Anthropologists on Art." In: *Readings in Anthropology* Vol. 2, *Cultural Anthropology,* edited by Morton H. Fried, pp. 478–490. Thomas Y. Crowell Company, New York, N.Y.

Tryk, Sheila. 1979. "Solving the Pecos Pottery Mystery." *New Mexico Magazine* 57, (No. 7). 20–23. Santa Fe.

Turner, Christy G., II, and Lofgren, Laurel. 1966. "Household Size of Prehistoric Western Pueblo Indians." *Southwestern Journal of Anthropology* 22 (No. 2): 117–132. Albuquerque, N. Mex.

Warren, A. H. 1968. "Petrographic Notes on Glaze-Paint Pottery." In: *The Cochiti Dam Archaeological Salvage Project, Part I: Report on the 1963 Season,* assembled by Charles H. Lange. *Museum of New Mexico Research Records,* (No. 6): 184–197. Santa Fe.

Washburn, Dorothy Koster. 1977. "A Symmetry Analysis of Upper Gila Area Ceramic Design." *Papers of the Peabody Museum of Archaeology and Ethnology* (No. 68). Cambridge, Mass.

Weaver, Donald E., Jr. 1978. *Prehistoric Population Dynamics and Environmental Exploitation in the Manuelito Canyon District, Northwestern New Mexico.* Ph.D. dissertation, Arizona State University, Tempe.

Wendorf, Fred. 1953. "Archaeological Studies in the Petrified Forest National Monument." *Museum of Northern Arizona Bulletin* (No. 27). Flagstaff.

Wilkinson, Nancy M. 1958. "Arts and Crafts of the Gallina Culture." *El Palacio* 65 (No. 5): 189–196. Santa Fe, N. Mex.

Wilson, L. W. W. 1918. "Hand Sign or Avanyu, A Note on a Pajaritan Biscuit-Ware Motif." *American Anthropologist* n.s., 20 (No. 3): 310–317. Lancaster, Pa.

Wobst, H. Martin. 1977. "Stylistic Behavior and Information Exchange." *Michigan Anthropological Papers* 61: 317–342. Ann Arbor, Mich.

Woodbury, Richard B., and Woodbury, Nathalie, F. S. 1956. "Zuñi Prehistory and El Morro National Monument." *Southwestern Lore* 21 (No. 4): 56–60. Boulder, Colo.

———. 1966. "Decorated Pottery of the Zuñi Area." In: *The Excavation of Hawikuh, by Frederick Webb Hodge, Appendix II. Contributions from the Museum of the American Indian, Heye Foundation* Vol. 20. New York, N.Y.

Zaslow, Bert, and Dittert, Alfred E., Jr. 1977a. "Pattern Theory Used as an Archaeological Tool: A Preliminary Statement." *Southwestern Lore* 43 (No. 1): 18–34. Boulder, Colo.

———. 1977b. "The Pattern Technology of the Hohokam." In: *Pattern Mathematics and Archaeology. Arizona State University Anthropological Research Papers* (No. 2). Tempe.